"*The Socially Confident Teen* is a practical, nonthreatening guide for teens to examine both their outside world of relationships with others, as well as their inside world of relationship with themselves to make sense of it in a way that will bring health and wellness to their mind and spirit. Christina Reese gently leads youth through valuable exercises taken at their own pace. I highly recommend it!"

—**Elaine C. Shenk, MS**, director of adoption/post adoption at
Bethany Christian Services of Central Pennsylvania

"*The Socially Confident Teen* is an excellent resource that can be used within a therapeutic setting and personal growth setting. Reese has provided a clear and practical workbook for teens to gain the skills needed to build healthy connections and relationships with others while facing the challenges of being a teenager in the world."

—**Carmen Jimenez-Pride, LCSW, RPT-S**, director of Outspoken Counseling and Consulting, LLC; and creator of Focus on Feelings books and resources

"This is a book I wish I had read as a teenager! Centered around the four attachment styles, Reese expertly provides a valuable resource to help guide teens through a very sensitive time of life. With its relatable case examples and a wealth of personal reflective exercises, teens are empowered to learn healthy strategies to engage in attuned interpersonal relationships with peers and others. A must-have resource for every therapist's bookshelf!"

—**Janet A. Courtney, PhD**, founder of FirstPlay Therapy, and author of
Healing Child and Family Trauma through Expressive and Play Therapies

"*The Socially Confident Teen* is an incredibly useful, well-written workbook for readers to use both on their own and for clinicians to use as a guide to work with patients. It is an easy-to-read, clear explanation of attachment and its impact on functioning, as well as relationships. Families will find this workbook useful to understand each other and their relationships. Further, it will help clinicians have a guide in working with attachment and building teen confidence and self-esteem. I cannot recommend this book highly enough!"

> —**Cynthia Welsh, LCSW- C, QCSW**, psychotherapist for twenty-two years; clinical supervisor; and founder of Alma Counseling, LLC

"Christina Reese's *The Socially Confident Teen* addresses one of the most significant aspects of adolescent life: relationships. It offers space for readers to look closely at how they function in their personal relationships, understand how these patterns developed, and learn what they can do to make their relationships as healthy and positive as possible. This is always an important goal, but even more so in a world where so much of a teen's social life is channeled through social media, and where cyber relationships color or take the place of in-person interaction. A well-organized and well-thought-out manual for social success, which can be helpful for adults as well!"

> —**Lisa M. Schab, LCSW**, psychotherapist; and author of nineteen self-help books, including *The Self-Esteem Workbook for Teens* and the guided journal, *Put Your Worries Here*

the socially confident teen

an attachment theory workbook to help you feel good about yourself & connect with others

CHRISTINA REESE, PhD

Instant Help Books
An Imprint of New Harbinger Publications, Inc.

Publisher's Note

Distributed in Canada by Raincoast Books

Copyright © 2022 by Christina Reese
     Instant Help Books
     An imprint of New Harbinger Publications, Inc.
     5674 Shattuck Avenue
     Oakland, CA 94609
     www.newharbinger.com

Cover design by Amy Shoup

Acquired by Jennye Garibaldi

Edited by Jennifer Holder

Library of Congress Cataloging-in-Publication Data on file

Printed in the United States of America

24 23 22

10 9 8 7 6 5 4 3 2 1   First Printing

This book is dedicated to my loving husband, Michael, who shares me with my computer while I am writing. And to my daughter, Lina, who recently traveled this road of teen attachment.

I love you both!

contents

foreword

Attachment theory has gained renewed prominence over the past two decades in psychotherapy, partly because of the popularity of neuroscience and the interpersonal neurobiological approach primarily linked with Daniel Siegel, MD, and Allan Schore at UCLA. Neuroscience findings have validated a lot of what we understood from the much earlier work of Freud on the significance of the mother-child relationship, further expanded by Daniel Stern in his groundbreaking 1985 book *The Interpersonal World of the Infant*. Around the same time, John Bowlby was writing about attachment and loss in England. I think his work would have had more impact if it were not for the British emphasis on object relations theory, with its mechanistic language presenting a barrier to American readers. In addition, there has been increasing emphasis in recent years on relational cultural writings from the Stone Center at Wellesley College led by Jean Baker Miller, MD, and Judith Jordan, PhD, among other seminal writers and thinkers. There has also been increasing emphasis on relational theory and therapies in general, in reaction to what many considered, an overemphasis on strictly cognitive-based approaches that have predominated, especially in academia where clinicians get their first indoctrination in the field.

What has been mostly lacking in the increasingly rich literature surrounding attachment theory are practical, clinical applications of the rather abstract theory, particularly as articulated by the British theorists when they talk about internal working models and concepts such as self-object and other-object. In this regard, this book by Christina Reese is not only based on positive psychology and empowerment, it is also a practical guide in the form of a workbook for teens to develop social confidence and become more securely attached in their relationships with family, friends, and their peer group. Particularly helpful is the author's guide to healthy relationships among peers and in dating relationships that pose such a risk to today's youth, especially if they did not benefit from secure relationships early in life with their primary attachment figures.

The challenge of engaging teens today, with all the competing demands from stimuli provided by social media with all its hazards, is enormous. Because of the bombardment of stimuli from social media and video games, many teens are unable to willfully apply their attention to tasks that don't razzle and dazzle them and virtually capture their attention. In addition to engagement with a task, persevering on a task that may not be of high interest—such as certain schoolwork and homework assignments—represents another significant challenge.

The author tries to make exercises in this workbook more inviting to teens by giving examples of scenarios that teens can relate to, having encountered them in daily life. The workbook exercises invite them to reflect on their attachment styles and the attachment styles of significant others with whom they interact. Great credit goes to the author for outlining the steps for teens to move toward secure attachment, regardless of what limiting attachment style they currently predominantly use. She explains all this in language teens can understand and absorb, a major achievement in and of itself. In my opinion, a book like this has been needed in our field for a long time and it couldn't be timelier.

—David A. Crenshaw, PhD, ABPP
    Author, licensed and board-certified clinical psychologist

dear parents and helping professionals

For more than a decade of a child's life, the parent is their primary attachment figure. The parent meets their needs, and protects and loves them. A child needs you to be their safe place, their home base, and their comfort zone to return to when the world is unkind, and unsupportive, or they crash-land after poor choices. As a primary attachment figure, you provide a safe place when the world is a hard place.

You have given them a model, an internal framework, about how relationships work. Their first relationship was with you! You most likely interacted with them in the same way that your parents interacted with you, for attachment styles are generational. Your foundational relationship is the template they will use to measure all future relationships. There are four types of relationship templates, or attachment styles: *secure, anxious ambivalent, avoidant,* and *disorganized.* Attachment begins in childhood between a parent and child, shifts during the teen years to peers, and grows in adulthood to significant others and friends. As you and your child navigate this teenage shift in attachment, may this book be a resource to support your journey.

In normal development, your teen begins looking outside the family for support and a safe place. In the years to come, peers will provide friendships and even romantic relationships. It is important that the people your child spends time with are positive and safe peers who will support them in reaching their goals. As your child searches for social circles where they belong, peers can make or break the teen years. Steering your child through the process of choosing healthy friends can be an important foundational part of the attachment shift during this time. One of the ways you can support them in their search for independence is by making sure they have a good understanding of attachment, or relationship building.

This book can help strengthen your child's peer relationships, increase their social success, and reinforce safety and support in family relationships. We all have needs: food, shelter, safety, and love. Love is a need met through relationships. When we have relationships that offer a sense of safety, we feel valued and respected, heard and seen, understood and supported. This leads to good mental health. When we face a struggle in life, we know we'll have the support to weather it. Relationships provide problem solving and comfort that will help us overcome struggles and be resilient.

However, without safe and healthy relationships, we feel disconnected and our relationships are dysfunctional. Our mental health suffers. We do not have validation and value, we do not have our need for love met. When we face distress in life, we are likely to be diagnosed with disorders like anxiety and depression because we feel too alone to face challenges. Having strong, healthy relationships where trust and vulnerability are present protects us from mental illness. Those same relationships can provide support and encouragement if your child ever does face a mental health struggle.

The first part of this book focuses on helping your child assess and understand their attachment style. It builds understanding about how their attachment style developed and shares the strengths and weaknesses that result. Then, for insecure attachment styles, it offers steps to move toward secure, healthy attachment. It may be helpful for your child to read through each attachment style to better understand other people they meet, as each style tends to view relationships differently. Attachment can also change based on the person we are attaching to, as the styles are fluid.

The second part of this book offers interventions to lead your child toward secure attachment. This develops your child's foundational understanding of relationships and what they can provide in a healthy context. Relationships involve attunement, or the meeting of each other's needs mutually, which builds trust. Understanding how trust is built, and how to repair it when it has been lost, is an essential relationship skill. Your child will explore how to share vulnerability appropriately, based in trust, to avoid heartbreak. This can increase self-esteem and provide protection from the risky emotional vulnerability that can lead to depression and anxiety. Sections address each of the insecure attachment styles, sharing what your child can do to work on relationship skills that develop healthy attachment. Concepts that impact relationships, like compromise, respect, boundaries, emotion regulation, and self-control, are explored. These healthy relationship skills will allow your child to grow secure attachments.

The third part focuses on specific relationships including friendships, dating, and the parent-child relationship. When your child can apply what they have learned about attachment to all their relationships, social success results. Replicating secure attachment in all environments ensures their needs for love and relationship are met in ways that preserve their mental health. Healthy attachment is for everyone!

dear reader

The teen years can be challenging for you, as they bring many changes. One of the major changes happening for you right now is a shift in the focus of your relationships, or attachments. For your whole life, your parents have been your primary attachment. This means they are the ones you most likely turn to for support, problem solving, or to be your safe place when life feels hard. Your parents taught you about relationships through modeling and by having a relationship with you. Attachment is generational, so your parents connected to you in the same way their parents connected to them. The four attachment styles that all relationships fall into are:

Secure Attachment: Feeling safe in relationships and returning to those connections for comfort, support, and problem solving. The secure attachment equation is *Trust + Attunement = Vulnerability.*

Anxious Attachment: Feeling insecure in relationships. You are doing more work than the other person and having anxiety that the relationship will not be there when you need it. *Trust* is missing from the secure attachment equation.

Avoidant Attachment: Feeling disconnected in relationships. Because everyone is independent and self-sufficient, you do not need to use relationships for comfort, security, support, or problem solving. *Attunement* is missing from the secure attachment equation.

Disorganized Attachment: Feeling that relationships are not safe places, cannot be trusted, and provide hurt and harm. While there is a need to feel close to others, there is also hesitancy about developing connections. *Vulnerability* is missing from the secure attachment equation.

You may, or may not, know how to have a relationship with your parents. You may, or may not, have confidence in how that relationship works and what it requires of you. Either way, now you are focusing on friendships and building relationships outside your family. This is normal and something every teenager begins to do. New friendships can be very different from the relationship you've had with your parents and family members for more than a decade. Knowing how to build friendships in healthy ways that create strong connections can lead to more satisfying relationships and social success throughout your life. This includes being able to express your needs and wants in ways others will hear and understand, choosing friends who will support your goals, and managing emotions in healthy ways. In this workbook, you will find activities that share how to build satisfying relationships and give you the chance to practice voicing your needs, identifying positive friends who support you, as well as expressing and calming your emotions.

This book explains the important foundational parts of attachment-based relationships and how they build on each other. It will help you recognize your needs, meet the needs of others, and allow others to meet your needs too. You can build trust with others and be trustworthy for your friends. Growing social skills, like respect and compromise, will increase your ability to be successful and feel confident with others. You'll even explore special relationships, like dating, and learn what these relationships may require in addition to foundational skills. Most of all, you'll learn more about *you*, including what is important to you in relationships, the strengths you can offer, and who you are becoming as a young adult.

Welcome to this attachment journey. Let's get started!

what is a healthy and fulfilling relationship?

Now that you are reaching outside your family for connection, you may have some ideas about what a relationship is and how to interact in one. Relationships can make us feel secure and connected. When we are in healthy relationships with others, we feel seen and heard, and our thoughts and emotions are validated. We matter to someone else and we have value. These are just a few things relationships provide and why we are healthier when we are connected to others.

Let's start by looking at some reasons why relationships are so important in your life. The reasons in this list are true now and will be true throughout your life. Building attachment skills now can help you feel healthy and fulfilled in so many supportive ways.

Relationships meet your need for support. When you feel connected to other people, it helps you in many ways. When facing struggles, you don't feel so alone. It helps to have people solve problems with you. Your brain actually functions better when connected with the brains of others.

Relationships are where you experience love. This includes family members, maybe friends, and possibly someone who inspires romantic feelings in you.

Relationships are where you explore interests and hobbies together. Whether you find people with similar interests or different interests, they can introduce you to new things. Perhaps it's a new hobby to enjoy, or more resources for an activity you already love. You find people who like doing things together, whether playing sports, listening to music, or talking. You enjoy doing activities with someone.

Relationships are where you find someone to talk to about your life. Maybe you have a friend who you are talking to about dating or what you want to learn about after high school. Talking these things through with a friend can help you realize how you think and feel, yourself. This helps form your identity, who you are as a person.

Relationships are where you can trust someone to be honest with you. Sometimes this is hard because their honesty may not be something you want to hear. They might share that you need to work on your attitude or make better choices. Their honesty can help you make better choices and grow into the person you want to be: someone who is respectful, dependable, and kind.

Relationships give you a place to talk about your feelings with comfort and acceptance. When you feel safe in a relationship, you can talk to that person about things that make you feel frustrated, sad, happy, or silly. When you are having a good day, you can count on that person to help you celebrate. When you are having a sad day, you can look to that person to comfort you with kind words or hugs.

Relationships help you know who you are. The people you are in relationship with tell you honestly about your strengths and weaknesses. They help you see yourself from a different perspective so you can gain more self-awareness.

When you have a healthy relationship with someone, that relationship is built in four steps: attunement, trust, vulnerability, and attachment.

1. *Attunement* means you are "in tune" with someone else. When someone is attuned to you, they see you, listen to you, know you. Because they know you, they understand what you need and can meet your needs. People meet your needs because they care about you.

2. *Trust* forms when someone meets your needs consistently. You trust people who meet your needs and the relationship begins to feel safe and secure.

3. *Vulnerability* in the safety of the relationship is important so that you can share your thoughts and emotions. You know they will be respected and honored. The other person can also be vulnerable with you, sharing their thoughts and feelings, knowing you will respect and honor them. This deepens the relationship.

4. *Attachment* is the result. Secure attachment means you feel connected with another person. You can relax, allowing another person to know all of you without fearing they will judge or reject you. You can truly be yourself, knowing you will be respected and accepted.

When you experience a securely attached relationship, your self-worth and self-esteem grow as you understand that you are valuable and loved. This relationship becomes a safe place for you, where you can turn for support and comfort. You can create relationships like this to meet your needs, feel safe enough to be vulnerable, and receive respect and acceptance. You are valuable, so this is what I wish for you: healthy and fulfilling attachment-based relationships!

PART ONE

Assessing Your Attachment Style

Attachment is how you interact in relationships with other people. Identifying your attachment style, or the characteristics that describe your relationships, will help you better understand the strengths and weaknesses you have in relationships. Then you can learn new skills for your attachment style so your relationships become more fulfilling.

The healthy type of relationship is secure attachment. This means that when you connect to others, you find safety and security. You feel confident being yourself, knowing that you are accepted and respected. Your relationships provide love, support, and help with solving problems. Healthy, secure attachment is based in attunement, or meeting one another's needs. This builds trust and allows you to be vulnerable with someone.

Sometimes your relationships can be characterized by anxiety, causing you to feel insecure in the connection. This anxiety can be because of past relationships, when you learned an anxious way of attaching to others. In your relationships, it can feel difficult for you to trust others and feel safe in those connections. This can create a lack of confidence in your connections. You may doubt the strength and security of your relationships.

Your relationships may also be characterized by detachment, or a need to be independent. This is often the result of needing to meet your own needs. A building block of healthy attachment is attunement, or meeting each other's needs. When your needs have not been met by others, and you have met them for yourself, independence grows. Independence gets in the way of attunement, so growing trust and vulnerability are more challenging. This can make it hard to feel close and safe in relationships.

If relationships have not felt safe for you, you have been in relationships with unsafe people, or have experienced trauma, your relationships may be more disorganized. You want to be close and connected in relationships to meet your need for love. However, because you haven't felt safe in relationships, the thing you need is also the thing you fear. Finding the way to healthy relationships can bring healing after feeling unsafe in past connections.

A primary caregiver, who you have spent the most time with, is the person whose attachment style you most likely mirror. Attachment can also be fluid, depending on the person. Maybe you have a parent who is a safe place for you, and you are securely attached to them. You may have a grandparent who is harsh or unkind, and you do not feel emotionally safe with them, so your attachment to them is disorganized. Perhaps a friend is very independent and self-sufficient, so when you spend time with them you begin to mirror their avoidant attachment style. Your other parent may have an anxious attachment style and you often feel unsure about the relationship. In this way, you may also see yourself in the other attachment styles, depending on which relationship you are thinking about.

Once you have identified your attachment style, you will learn more about it in the following chapters. You will also do activities to learn more secure ways of relating. You may want to learn about the other attachment styles, because you will better understand friends and family members who have different styles of relating and connecting. You may recognize styles in people you know and interact with every day. By understanding them better, you may be able to improve your relationships with them and enjoy more satisfying connections.

Here is a quiz to assess your attachment style. For each statement in the following list, put a check mark in the column that says "This describes my relationships" or "This does not describe my relationships." At the end of the list, calculate a score that will identify your attachment style. You can take this quiz repeatedly to see what you are learning. Go to http://www.newharbinger.com/48725 to download a copy.

Attachment Style Quiz

	This statement describes my relationships	This statement does not describe my relationships
1. I value independence in relationships.		
2. I enjoy meeting the needs of others.		
3. I worry others will leave me.		
4. I have a hard time trusting others.		
5. I feel safe and find comfort in relationships.		
6. I think each person should meet their own needs.		
7. I turn to relationships for help to solve problems.		
8. I feel my relationships are not very strong.		
9. I have a hard time knowing where limits are in relationships.		
10. I want my needs to be met by others.		
11. I have relationships, but do not feel close to anyone.		
12. I think my needs are more important than others' needs.		
13. I have a hard time being vulnerable.		
14. I do not feel valued by others.		
15. I want to meet my own needs.		
16. I feel accepted for who I am.		
17. I want others to do things my way.		
18. I cannot identify with the feelings of others.		
19. I feel like I have to work hard to keep my relationships.		
20. I need to control other people in my relationships.		

Now it's time to calculate your score to identify your attachment style. For each question number, if you checked the box "This describes my relationships," make one mark in the "Score" column. Then count your marks, write in the total, and circle the attachment style that has the highest score.

Question number	Score	Attachment style
2, 5, 7, 10, 16	. Total: _____	Secure
3, 8, 14, 19, 20	Total: _____	Anxious
1, 4, 6, 13, 15	Total: _____	Avoidant
9, 12, 11, 17, 18	Total: _____	Disorganized

The style you circled, because it has the most points, is likely your attachment style. The rest of this book describes more about each attachment style and offers activities you can do to gain skills for forming more secure attachments. It will be helpful for you to read all of them so you can better understand how your way of connecting in relationships may be different from the way others are connecting. Understanding our differences helps build healthier relationships.

1 secure attachment

for you to know

Secure attachment provides a safe place, a comfort zone. It is characterized by a relationship that validates your feelings, and helps you feel valued and accepted. It offers you a place to solve problems and a refuge from the world around you.

Jordan and Michael are both seniors and share a lot of the same classes. They are on the football team and look forward to away games so they can talk on the bus. Their conversations often evolve into debates because they have opposing views on almost every topic they talk about. However, their debates are characterized by respect and understanding. Jordan presents his views and beliefs while Michael listens and tries to understand his friend's point of view. Michael does the same when Jordan is talking. They both feel able to be honest, share their real thoughts and feelings, and trust each other to offer acceptance and respect.

Secure attachment is a way of relating to others that has a healthy balance: needs are met, respect is offered, and care is felt. It provides a safe place to relax in, emotionally and physically. You can feel free to share thoughts and feelings, knowing that you will be respected and validated. You return to the relationship when you need comfort and connection. This gives you the strength and motivation to leave again, heading out into the world to try again. If you have a different attachment style, then understanding what secure attachment is like and what it involves can help you to move toward having healthier relationships.

for you to do

Your relationship with your parents is your first experience of connection. Their example for how a relationship works is what you will know and believe about relationships. It shapes your own relating skills. Think about the relationship that you have with your parents and answer the following questions.

How have your parents met your physical and emotional needs?

_____

_____

_____

Do you trust your parents? If so, what do you trust them with? Is there anything that you do not trust them with?

_____

_____

_____

Are you able to share your thoughts and feelings with your parents? Do you feel that your experience is valued and respected? Does this make it easier or harder to share new thoughts and feelings with them?

_____

_____

_____

Do you feel your parents provide you with a safe place, refuge, or comfort zone from the world around you? If so, what are the ways they make this space for you?

_____

_____

_____

Are you able to leave home and go out into the world with confidence and purpose? If so, what do your parents do to encourage that confidence and purpose?

_____

_____

_____

more to do

Now think about relationships outside your parents and family. How do you use the following characteristics of secure attachment in relationships with others (friends, classmates, teachers, coaches)? Answer the questions by describing things you do and say.

How do you meet the needs of others?

_____

_____

_____

How do you know you can trust others? How do you encourage them to trust you?

_____

_____

_____

How do you feel about sharing your thoughts and feelings with others?

_____

_____

_____

What is their response when you share those thoughts and feelings? Do you receive validation and support?

_____

_____

_____

What relationships provide you with a safe place, refuge, or comfort zone? Have you found any friends or adults (other than your parents) who create this space for you?

_____

_____

_____

Do you have friends or other adults who encourage you to go out into the world to pursue your goals? How do they encourage you to do this?

_____

_____

_____

for you to do

No matter your attachment style, by assessing the characteristics of secure attachment that you already have, and those that you need to develop, you can create a plan for how to move toward secure attachment. If you already have secure attachments, recognizing what makes them secure can help you recognize someone with a different attachment style. You might mirror their style in an effort to connect to them. Be mindful of this, as secure attachment is healthy attachment. Instead of changing to connect to someone with a different style that may not be as healthy, you can maintain your secure attachment. This encourages them to connect to you based on healthy attachment. In this way, you may help them create stronger and more fulfilling relationships.

Think about the following statements to explore secure attachment. If a statement is true for you, check the box next to it.

- ☐ I express my needs using words.

- ☐ I seek comfort in friends and family.

- ☐ I feel my home and family are my safe place.

- ☐ I meet the needs of others.

- ☐ I look for others to meet my needs.

- ☐ I like solving problems with others.

- ☐ I can share my thoughts and feelings with others, and my experience is respected.

- ☐ I build trust easily with others.

- ☐ I am in relationships that feel safe.

- ☐ I have relationships with others who share my relationship values.

If you checked each box, then you have secure attachments. If you did not check many boxes, these are things you can work on learning and developing in order to find *earned* secure attachment. It is called "earned" because, if you did not experience a securely attached relationship with your primary caregiver, you will need to work to achieve this type of a relationship. The important thing to remember is that secure attachments, even if they require work to achieve, are worth the effort. They provide emotional safety and connections that are satisfying and meaningful.

2 anxious attachment

for you to know

An anxious attachment style can create discomfort in connection because you feel insecure in relationships. You feel you must work extra hard in relationships to keep people engaged. You may fear others will leave you because you do not have enough to offer in the relationship.

Ally struggles to feel confident in relationships. She often asks her friends if they like her new outfits. She feels jealous if her friends talk to other people. She worries that if they have others to enjoy spending time with, they might stop spending time with her. Ally is anxious about losing her friends, so she is always planning fun activities and wanting them to hang out with her all the time. She doesn't like being by herself and feels insecure when talking to her friends. Ally can't tell them what she really thinks about things because she is worried they won't like her anymore. Sometimes relationships feel exhausting to her.

Your parents may frequently worry about your safety or whether you are being treated fairly. They may intervene in social and academic situations to make sure you are okay. As a result, you may feel you need others to take care of you. This can unintentionally give you the message that you cannot handle life or the world surrounding you. It can teach you that someone else needs to speak for you or help you get your needs met. This can impact your self-esteem and self-confidence, causing you to struggle with recognizing your strengths. It is important to remember that you do have strengths. You can feel calm and confident in relationships by finding earned secure attachment.

for you to do

Think about how your first relationship, with your parents, shaped and molded your beliefs about how relationships work. Think about the relationship skills they taught you through what they've said and done.

If your parents helped you a lot and intervened on your behalf in childhood, what did this communicate to you about your ability to manage yourself? How do you feel about this?

_____

_____

_____

What do you think motivated your parents to care for your needs in this way?

_____

_____

_____

What are the activities (such as completing applications, negotiating with teachers, talking to friends) that you feel you need help with? Are these activities that you need parents to do with or for you?

_____

_____

_____

Consider your list of activities. Circle any that you can try to do yourself. What are some small steps you can take to begin using your own voice and advocating for yourself?

_____

_____

_____

How might your parents respond to this? Write down some ways you can communicate that you are ready to use your own voice.

_____

_____

_____

more to do

Now think about relationships you have outside of your family. How are your current beliefs about relationships impacting those attachments? Consider whether they are helping or harming your connections with others.

Does your anxiety in relationships impact your friendships positively or negatively? How does your anxiety show up when you are with others?

_____

_____

_____

How do your friends respond when you express anxiety or low confidence? Does this make them feel closer to you or further from you?

_____

_____

_____

Healthy relationships are characterized by balance in meeting each other's needs emotionally, physically, and mentally. Is there balance in your friendships? Do you need others as much as they need you? Or more? Or less?

_____

_____

_____

How would your relationships change if you were more confident and secure in those connections? Would the relationships stay the same, grow stronger, or get weaker?

_____

_____

_____

What are at least two strengths you have that you use in relationships (such as kindness, generosity, creativity, being a good listener, responsibility, dependability, honesty, humor, healthy communication, loyalty, forgiveness, patience, teamwork, compromise)? There are probably more than two! If you can think of more, write them down.

_____

_____

_____

Consider the following statements and place a check beside the ones you feel describe you.

☐ I feel that I must work hard to maintain relationships.

☐ I work harder in relationships than others.

☐ I worry that friends will leave the relationship.

☐ I think I do not have a lot to offer in relationships and worry that others will realize this.

☐ I need relationships to feel valued.

☐ I do not like to spend time alone.

☐ I struggle with confidence.

☐ I have a hard time identifying two strengths that I have.

☐ I do not rest and relax in relationships.

☐ I avoid arguments and disagreements.

If you checked most of these boxes, you may have an anxious attachment style. It is possible to increase your confidence and security in relationships. It will take work to change the way you are relating to others. The effort is worth it when you experience the safety and security that healthy relationships provide.

You have strengths and contributions that you offer within relationships that others value. Having confidence in those and focusing on controlling your anxiety and emotions, instead of trying to control the other person, will increase the strength of your relationships. In this workbook, focus on the activities in parts two and three to earn secure attachment and address anxious attachment. You will learn more about how you can find healthy relationships.

for you to know

An avoidant attachment style is characterized by fierce independence, self-sufficiency, and lack of trust. You may feel great pressure to continue to apply these characteristics, which can create feelings of anxiety and depression if you cannot maintain your independence.

Meg's parents are always busy, so at an early age she learned to take care of herself and her own needs. She comes home from school, completes her homework, and fixes herself dinner. Then she plays video games or watches television until she falls asleep. She is independent and self-sufficient. She doesn't need anyone's help, and also doesn't offer anyone help either.

When Meg connected with Kyle during a school project, he constantly offered to give her a ride home after school. But she preferred to take care of herself and walk home. He offered to help her with some challenging homework, but Meg always did it herself and felt proud when she figured it out on her own. One day, the assignment was so hard that she accepted his offer. Kyle was able to explain it in a way that made sense to her. Meg discovered it feels good to know she is not alone in her struggles. Having someone to solve problems with, who cares about her success, feels like a relief. Meg is now learning to have a different type of relationship than what she was used to in the past, because she likes the type of relationship that Kyle is offering her.

Avoidant attachment is characterized by independence and self-sufficiency. You may want to take care of yourself, and probably have for a long time. This can lead to avoiding deep and vulnerable connections with others. Avoiding your own needs, and the needs of others, may be the way you function in relationships. You might feel uncomfortable when others express vulnerability because you are uncomfortable with your own vulnerability. Because you doubt that if you express your thoughts and feelings, they will be validated and respected, you find it easier to withhold them from others. This results in a lack of trust in relationships. Rather than giving and taking, you feel each person should be self-sufficient and independent. Remember that secure attachment can be earned when you are able to connect with others using attunement and trust. Once you feel safe in the relationship, you can also be vulnerable.

for you to do

Think of the relationship you have had with your parents over the years. Consider how the relationship skills they modeled have developed in you by answering the following questions.

What is your first memory of taking care of your own needs or emotions? How do you feel about this?

_____

_____

_____

What may have caused your parents to encourage your early independence (such as long work hours, hobbies, distractions from parenting, or valuing independence as a personality trait)?

_____

_____

_____

Consider your relationship with your parents now. Are you able to share thoughts and feelings with them, and receive acceptance and validation? If not, could you talk to them about this?

_____

_____

_____

Often your parents are parenting you in the same way they were parented. This may be how your grandparents had a relationship with your parents, so now they are having the same type of relationship with you. Knowing this, how do you feel about your parents and the relationship modeling they gave you? Would you choose a more secure style?

_____

_____

_____

What are some ways that you wish your relationship with your parents was different? Can you talk to them about this?

_____

_____

_____

more to do

Think about the relationships you have outside of your immediate family, with friends and other adults. How do your beliefs about relationships impact those connections, both positively and negatively? Consider this as you answer the following questions.

When your friends talk about what they need or express emotions, how does that make you feel?

_____

_____

_____

If you shared your own emotions or needs with them, what do you think their reactions would be?

_____

_____

_____

Being vulnerable takes a lot of courage. Describe a time when you were courageous about showing your vulnerability. Can you use that same courage to share needs or emotions with a friend? You have courage inside you and you can use it in your relationships too!

_____

_____

_____

Feeling safe in a relationship and sharing emotions creates a deeper bond and connection. What are some of the positive and negative sides to this kind of relationship?

_____

_____

_____

To be vulnerable requires trust. Write down the names of people you trust. Then identify the percentage points that reflect how much you trust each of them. For example, you may share 10 percent of your thoughts with one person and share 50 percent of your emotions with another person. What do you share with them, and how much do you share?

_____

_____

_____

Consider the following statements and place a checkmark beside the ones that you feel describe your relationships.

☐ I like to be independent.

☐ I take care of my own needs.

☐ I expect others to be independent too.

☐ I take care of my feelings instead of sharing them.

☐ I expect others to take care of their needs.

☐ I expect others to contain their feelings.

☐ I see vulnerability as a weakness.

☐ I do not trust others easily.

☐ When someone loses my trust, I do not give them another chance to earn it.

☐ I like to have things my way.

If you checked most of these boxes, you may have an avoidant attachment style. All teenagers are working hard to be independent and show that they can take care of more of their own needs and wants. It's important to recognize that, on the relationship spectrum, *dependence* is at one end and *independence* is at the other end. Neither extreme is healthy. Instead, we strive for balance in the middle, which is *interdependence*, in healthy relationships. Finding that balance is secure attachment, with relationships characterized by feeling emotionally safe enough to be vulnerable and share your truest self with others. Working to achieve this may include learning to recognize the needs of others and then meeting those needs in order to build trust. However, it will also involve learning to communicate your own needs so that others can meet them and earn your trust. In this workbook, focus on the activities in parts two and four to learn about secure attachment and address avoidant attachment.

4 disorganized attachment

for you to know

A disorganized attachment style is created when you are searching for safety and security in a relationship, but instead find harm and hurt. When you have a disorganized attachment style, you continue to try to connect with someone but each attempt at connection ends in pain and rejection. This causes you to fear one of the strongest needs everyone has: relationships.

R.J. grew up with a father who drank alcohol too much. His father came home from work, began drinking, and then often became a mean parent. He yelled at R.J. or his mother. Sometimes he hit them. R.J. and his mother moved out of the house, and his parents have been divorced for several years. He rarely sees his father, but wishes they could have a closer relationship. During basketball, he sees other fathers at games to cheer for their kids. He hears friends talk about fishing with their dads or going on family vacations. R.J. wants to do things with his father too, but for a long time R.J. was too afraid to ask him. When he did rouse the courage to suggest it, his dad said he was too busy. But R.J. knew all his father did was work and drink. As a result, R.J. is too afraid to ask his friends to hang out with him on the weekends. He is worried they will be too "busy" or not interested. He thinks that, if his friends are anything like his father, it may be better not to ask them at all.

This relationship style follows an experience of a relationship that was not safe either physically or emotionally. It is difficult to begin the process of healing unless we feel safe. No one should feel unsafe in their home or immediate family situation. Safety is a need that everyone has. If you are still in an unsafe situation, choose an adult who you trust (your doctor, teacher, or another family member). Then share the reasons that you don't feel safe. Once you are in a place where you feel safe, these steps to learn about healthy relationships will support your emotional safety.

In your relationships now, you may have a hard time connecting with others. You may want to connect, but not know how. Your parents and caregivers modeled relationships for you and offered examples for how to connect. But because the primary adults in your life showed you that hurt and rejection were normal in relationships, you may feel confused now that you are trying to form your own connections with others. We all tend to repeat what was modeled for us, even if we do not want to. So you may find yourself hurting and rejecting others in the same way that you were hurt and rejected. This does not help your relationships grow. In fact, it may quickly end relationships you want to keep. You did not choose the relationship skills you were taught as a child, but you do have the ability to now learn new skills. They can lead you to satisfying and deeply intimate connections that you may have been seeking your whole life and have yet to find.

for you to do

Think about the relationships you had with your parents and caregivers in childhood. They shaped your understanding of relationships now. Then answer the following questions.

What parts of past relationships have been most hurtful to you? How do those experiences impact your relationships now?

_____

_____

_____

We all long for connections with others that feel safe and secure. What do you long for in a relationship?

_____

_____

_____

What would it feel like to find this type of a safe and secure connection with another person?

_____

_____

_____

Who would you like to have this type of a relationship with? A family member? A friend?

_____

_____

_____

The pain of past relationships can be a barrier to finding love and safety in future relationships. But it doesn't have to be. Write about why you would like to learn new skills for connecting with people and what this would mean to you.

_____

_____

_____

more to do

Consider each of the relationship terms in this section and write what they mean to you. Write your experience of each one, positive or negative. Then challenge yourself to change the way you think about each one by learning more about them and doing the exercises in this book.

When I hear the word "relationship," I think: _____

_____

When I hear the word "trust," I think: _____

_____

When I hear the word "needs," I think: _____

_____

When I hear the word "vulnerability," I think: _____

_____

When I hear the word "feelings," I think: _____

_____

When I hear the word "acceptance," I think: _____

_____

When I hear the word "compromise," I think: _____

_____

When I hear the word "respect," I think: _____

_____

When I hear the word "boundaries," I think: _____

_____

When I hear the word "empathy," I think: _____

_____

When I hear the word "comfort," I think: _____

_____

When I hear the words "safe place," I think: _____

_____

Read the following statements and place a checkmark next to the ones that you feel describe your relationships.

☐ I feel uncomfortable when people share their emotions with me.

☐ I can have a hard time managing my own emotions in relationships.

☐ My relationships do not last long.

☐ I do not feel close to anyone.

☐ I want to have close relationships, but they don't seem to work out.

☐ I struggle to honor others' relationship requests.

☐ Relationships do not feel like safe places to me.

☐ I do not always recognize the strengths of others.

☐ I feel that I need to protect myself in relationships.

☐ It is hard for me to trust and be vulnerable with others.

If you checked most of the boxes in this list, you may have a disorganized attachment style. This means you want to have relationships with others, but struggle to know how. In your life experience, relationships may not have felt like safe places. It may be hard to now imagine that relationships can feel satisfying, fulfilling, and meaningful. But they can! It may take perseverance and determination to create healthy relationships. Know that you already have those character traits if you endured relationships that didn't feel safe. Refocusing these traits can help you find safety and security in relationships now. It's well worth your time and effort when you experience all that relationships are meant to be! As you do the exercises in this workbook, focus on parts two and five. The activities explain secure attachment and offer a path to travel from a disorganized attachment style to healthy relationships.

PART TWO

The Pathway to Earning Secure Attachment

5 in tune with you!

for you to know

Being "in tune" with yourself and others feels good. The experience relies on a skill you can learn: attunement. In healthy relationships, attunement is meeting each other's needs equally and mutually. Needs include love, emotional support (coping and calming feelings), physical support (food, shelter, clothing), and mental support (problem solving or thinking through a problem). Here's what attunement sounds like in a conversation between friends walking home from school.

"Hey, how was your day?" Paula asks.

"Fine," Deanna responds.

"What does 'fine' mean?" asks Paula, curiously.

"I don't know," Deanna says as her forehead wrinkles. Paula can see confusion in her friend's face.

"Well, are you happy about anything?" Paula offers to help her friend open up the conversation. "Frustrated by that hard history test? Disappointed that Sean was out sick today?" She winks to help put Deanna at ease.

"I really don't know," Deanna says with a blank look on her face. "I hadn't thought about it."

"Maybe you can think about how you're doing while we walk? Then tell me when we get to your house?" Paula asks as she challenges her friend to tune in and notice her own feelings.

Deanna nods and keeps walking. A few minutes later, she says, "I guess now that the history test is over, I feel relieved. And hopeful that I'll see Sean at school tomorrow." Both girls laugh and they start discussing the test questions that were hardest for them. The conversation during their walk home is fulfilling and enjoyable.

By knowing yourself better, and knowing what you need, then you are able to ask for it in a relationship. Deanna didn't know what she felt until Paula asked her, but once she thought for a few minutes, she did know her feelings! If other people are going to be in tune with you, you must first be in tune with yourself. Knowing yourself will help others get to know you too. Take a few minutes to consider what you know about yourself and write responses to the following questions.

What is the feeling that you feel most often? _____

When do you feel this emotion? Describe the times of day or what situations you are in when you feel it.

_____

_____

What are some thoughts that you don't like to have?

_____

Why don't you like these thoughts? Describe how they cause you to feel and act.

_____

_____

What helps you calm down when you are upset?

_____

When you don't have that resource, how long does it take you to calm down?

_____

When you have that resource, do you calm down more quickly? Why?

_____

These are just a few questions to get you started. It's important to know yourself: what makes you feel happy or sad, what activities you enjoy or avoid, and why. Then you can use this knowledge in your relationships. When you know your own thoughts and feelings, you can share them with others. You can ask others for things you need. For example, if you are struggling with an assignment, you can ask a friend, "Can I talk to you about a paper for my English class? I could use some help brainstorming a topic."

Knowing yourself well leads to insights about who you are. An identity develops when you become more aware of your thoughts and feelings, then are able to express them to others so they know who you are too. Within relationships, when you express your identity, you will find either acceptance and support, or dismissal and rejection. A securely attached relationship will accept and support your identity. Trust needs to be present in order for you to feel vulnerable enough to share these parts of yourself and feel emotionally safe.

for you to do

To develop insight into who you are and then build your identity, you can think in pictures. Take some time to think about the following prompts and questions, then draw the answers.

What is your greatest *need* in relationships at this moment? Draw a picture of it.

How can you have this need met?

_____

_____

_____

Draw your greatest *want* in relationships at this moment.

How can you work to *earn* what you want in relationships?

_____

_____

_____

Draw a picture of who you are *now,* a self-portrait.

What do you notice about this drawing? What does it say about you? Who are you in this picture?

_____

_____

_____

Draw a picture of yourself in *five* years. What will your life look like? What will you be doing? Who will be part of your life? Include these things in your picture.

Draw a picture of yourself in *ten* years. What will your life look like? What will you be doing? Who will be part of your life? Include these things in your picture.

Getting to know yourself better will help you share yourself with others and allow them to know who you are. Spend some time thinking about who you are now, what things are important to you, and who you want to be in the future. This will develop your identity. Figuring out who you want to be will give you a goal as you grow and mature into an adult. You will know what direction you want to move in as you create your adult life. Knowing what your needs are as you move forward allows you to ask people in relationship with you to help you meet those needs.

more to do

This week, notice your needs. Focus on what your needs are and how you meet them. Do you meet your needs yourself, or do others meet them? Record them in the following table.

My need	How I met my need myself	How someone else met my need
Food	I woke up late and was hungry, so I made breakfast for myself.	Dad made dinner tonight and the school made my lunch. I didn't tell them; they knew I had the need.
Love		Mom hugged me. My grandfather gave me a carving he made. I didn't ask for these things; they knew I would appreciate them.
Understanding	I knew I was upset, so I thought about what might help me calm down.	My best friend listened when I was upset. I told him that I just needed to vent.

Noticing how you get your needs met can help develop insight into how others are in tune with you to meet your needs. You will start to see how attunement happens. Recognize if you are both meeting your own needs *and* allowing others to meet some of your needs. If you have a hard time allowing others to meet your needs, think about what might be stopping you from trusting others to meet those needs. This is important because, as you'll explore in activity 8, when people meet your needs, trust develops.

attuned to others

for you to know

When you are connected to others and meeting another's needs, your brain benefits. It makes really important new connections, which grow to make you smarter and more resilient. We all become stronger when we are together!

Over the last several years, Sandy's relationship with her parents has been changing. As a baby, she was dependent on her parents. She could not take care of herself, feed herself, pay for her clothes, or transport herself to school. Now that Sandy is a teenager who can do so much more for herself, the relationship with her parents has become interdependent. Sandy works at a job several days a week and uses the money to buy clothes, pay for haircuts, and fund activities with friends. She helps her parents take care of the house on weekends, doing laundry, dusting, and gardening. When Sandy graduates from high school and moves to college, she will be independent, taking care of herself. She will work a part-time job, go to the grocery store to buy her own food, and take care of her own needs and wants.

Many relationships, like the one between Sandy and her parents, change over time and move through a spectrum of connection. In a healthy relationship, attunement is a two-way street and is foundational to building attachment. We meet each other's needs. If someone is meeting your needs, you can show appreciation and love by identifying their needs and trying to meet them. You can watch what they do, or listen to what they say, and find clues about their needs.

Relationships happen along a spectrum that has *dependence* and *independence* as extremes. In the middle is *interdependence*. Here's how you can visualize it.

Dependence	Interdependence	Independence

At one end are *dependent* relationships, in which one person relies on another person for everything. It is normal for a child to be dependent on their parents. When you were a baby, your parents met all your needs. They helped you with everything. They were attuned to you and took care of you because they love you. They knew when you needed to be fed and they fed you. How your parents met your needs when you were dependent on them influences the development of your attachment style.

As you grow and mature, you are able to do more things for yourself. You still need your parents to buy the groceries, but you can make snacks for yourself or even an occasional weekend breakfast for the family! As you stretch your wings and try flying a bit, your confidence and self-esteem grow as you see all the things you can do. Staying completely dependent on your parents, when you don't need to be, can reduce confidence and self-esteem. It's good to try new things!

At the other end of the spectrum is *independence*. This happens when you meet all your own needs. This is not healthy in a relationship because it removes attunement from relationship building. Without attunement, trust does not grow. Without trust, most relationships end. People who say they are independent are not aware of the needs that they cannot meet for themselves. Everyone depends on others to meet some of their needs. For example, the need for love can only be met by another. When we love ourselves, we may experience peace, but when another loves us, there is also validation, fulfillment, and joy.

As you grow older, you will explore a new type of relationship with your parents, in which you see each other's needs and meet them. When your parents come home from the store carrying heavy bags, do you help them bring in the groceries? Or when your parents are mowing the lawn in the summer, do you consider whether they might be thirsty? You can bring them a cold glass of iced tea. You can also be attuned to your friends. When you see them drop books and you help to pick them up, you are seeing what they need and caring enough to help them.

This is *interdependence* and being attuned to each other. It describes a healthy relationship in the middle of the spectrum. In an interdependent relationship, no one's needs are more important than someone else's needs. In the same way, no one's wants are more important than someone else's wants. Each person deserves to have their needs met. This develops attunement and trust in a relationship. When you know you can depend on someone and trust them to be there for you, the relationship becomes stronger. You are not focused on meeting your own needs; you are focused on meeting the needs of others, and they are focused on meeting your needs. Your needs are being met, but not only by you! This is how relationships grow deeper. You are interdependent.

for you to do

Pay attention to the needs of people around you: parents, siblings, teachers, friends, even someone at the grocery store. Then, using this chart, track the needs you saw or heard, and the needs you met.

Name	Need	How I noticed the need	Did I meet the need? If so, how?
My history teacher, Mr. Kerr	He was returning papers he graded and dropped them	I saw it	I helped him pick up the papers
My sister, Ella	A ride to her friend's house	My mom asked me to help	I drove her there

How did it feel to meet their needs?

_____

Becoming aware of the needs of those around you, and beginning to meet them, will help you connect and attach to the people around you. This helps you form healthy relationships. Stay curious about the needs of others.

more to do

Meeting the needs of others is the foundation of having good relationships. Recognizing the needs of others is the first step. Think of your family and friends, their needs, and how you may meet their needs. In each circle, write the name of a person in your life. Then list their needs, the ones that you already meet and the ones you want to meet. Remember that love is a need, so if you love someone by giving them hugs, encouraging them with kind words, spending quality time with them, or doing kind things for them, then you are meeting a need for love.

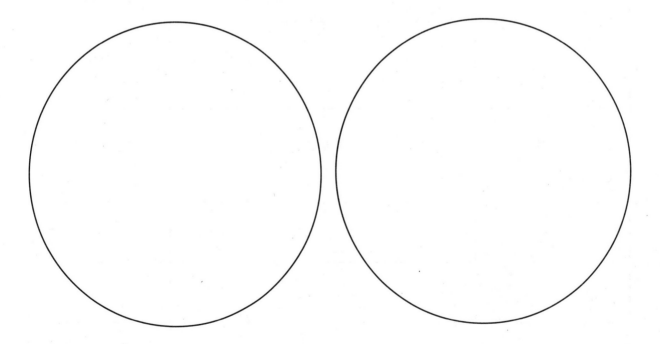

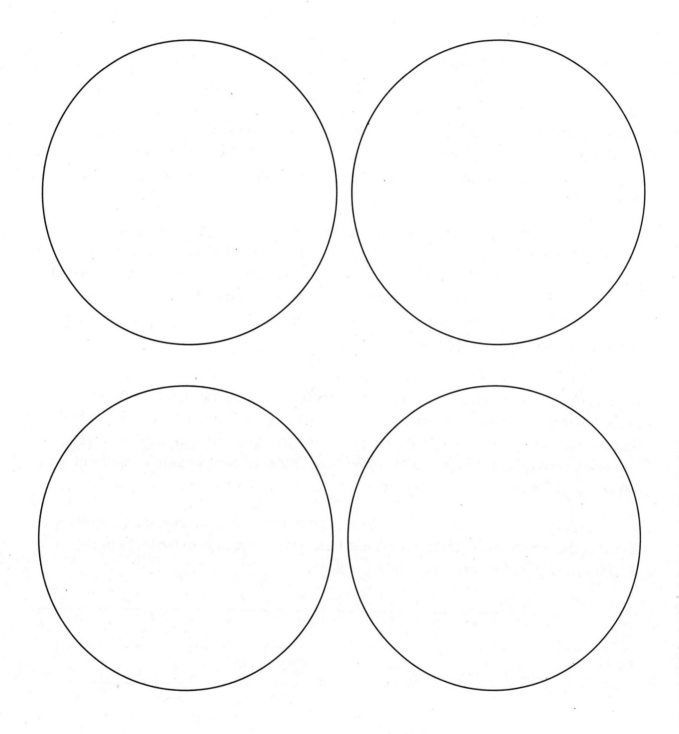

7 others in tune with you!

for you to know

Attunement is like a dance, with two people moving together to create something beautiful! Do you know how to dance in sync with others? Pause your reading and go online to look for a few videos of people dancing the waltz, the tango, or the jive. What do you notice?

In these dances, two people are moving together. One person leads and the other follows. Sometimes they take turns leading and following. When two people come together, meeting each other's needs, it looks like a beautiful dance. You respond to each other, respect each other, and communicate effectively. Both people can't lead at the same time. They have to take turns. In a relationship, leading is each person using their strengths to help the other person.

Maybe you and a friend are study buddies. They are great at science and you are great with math. So, they teach you science and you listen to learn. They are leading and you are following. Then you teach them math and they listen to learn. You are leading and they are following. You take turns. By appreciating the differences in each other, you will enjoy each other's strengths and support each other in your weaknesses. We all have strengths and weaknesses, things that are easy and hard for us.

Consider how you feel when you are leading and how you feel when you are following. If one or the other makes you feel uncomfortable, take some time to write about the discomfort and explore why you might feel it.

_____

_____

_____

Do you have any relationships that are one sided, where you are either meeting all the other person's needs, or they are meeting all of yours? Write down the names of people in one-sided relationships with you. Then check the box that applies.

Name	They meet all my needs (I am leading)	I meet all their needs (I am following)

Why are these one-sided relationships?

_____

_____

_____

What are strengths you have that you can offer to others?

_____

_____

_____

What are weaknesses you have that you need others to help overcome?

_____

_____

_____

What are some things you can do and say to balance these relationships?

_____

_____

_____

No one can meet all of their own needs. No one is good at everything. We all need others to help us with certain things—maybe not everything, but some things.

How do you feel about having needs that you cannot meet for yourself?

_____

_____

_____

When you have needs that you cannot meet for yourself, and you are not open to others meeting them for you, this impacts your ability to be everything that you have the potential to be! Your relationships will also be impacted. It is like dancing with someone who wants to lead all the time. The other person never gets a chance to lead, so they may decide to leave the dance. Similarly, if you follow all the time then no one gets to see your strengths or benefit from them.

Taking turns leading and following is a healthy dance and healthy attunement. When needs are mutually met, you can trust the other person and they trust can you. This opens the door for vulnerability and a deeper connection in the relationship.

for you to do

In this chart, list the needs you have that you cannot meet for yourself. Then identify who meets those needs for you. How do you feel when your needs are met? How do you feel about the person who is meeting those needs? This is when you are following, allowing another person's strengths to meet your needs.

Pay particular attention to the last column: how you feel about the person meeting your needs. This is how attunement feels and how trust then builds. These feelings are what cause you to trust the person who is meeting that need.

My need	Who meets my need and how they meet it	How I feel when this need is met	How I feel about the person meeting my need
A ride to work	My older sister drove me there	Happy because I can earn money at work	Thankful
Help with math homework	My friend Jenny helps me understand the concepts	Relieved because I don't have to figure it out by myself	Appreciative

My need	Who meets my need and how they meet it	How I feel when this need is met	How I feel about the person meeting my need

Now think about the dance of leading and following, you meeting the needs of others and them meeting your needs. In this chart, identify how this dance works in a relationship that is important to you. How do you meet each other's needs? How do you use your strengths and weaknesses to dance, to know when to lead and when to follow? Fill in the columns to explore your relationship.

Example: My Friend Sarah

How I meet their needs: I help her with science

How they meet my needs: She helps me write papers

Their strengths	Their weaknesses	My strengths	My weaknesses
She's very imaginative	She's not organized	I'm very organized	I can't think of new ideas

Example: My Cousin Tommy

How I meet their needs: I give him hugs that help calm him down

How they meet my needs: He gives me hugs and I feel appreciated

Their strengths	Their weaknesses	My strengths	My weaknesses
He's understanding and compassionate	Sometimes he gets really stressed out	I tackle challenges head on	I try to control people too much

My important relationship: _____

How I meet their needs: _____

How they meet my needs: _____

Their strengths	Their weaknesses	My strengths	My weaknesses

My important relationship: _____

How I meet their needs: _____

How they meet my needs: _____

Their strengths	Their weaknesses	My strengths	My weaknesses

My important relationship: _____

How I meet their needs: _____

How they meet my needs: _____

Their strengths	Their weaknesses	My strengths	My weaknesses

more to do

Once you know what you need, and you find a person who can meet the need, how do you let someone know what your need is? *How you ask* for their help can make all the difference. Think about something that you need and who you want to ask for help.

This is what I need: _____

This is who I want to ask for help with my need: _____

There are three different parts of voicing your needs: the volume of your voice, the tone of your voice, and the words you use. Think about each one.

> **Part 1:** You have different volumes: loud, medium, and soft. You can practice each one right now. Say, "I need something to eat" in each of those three volumes.
>
> How did each volume feel to you? _____
>
> _____
>
> _____
>
> When you ask someone to meet a need for you, which volume do you think they will want to respond to? _____
>
> **Part 2:** You have different tones: kind, demanding, and sarcastic. You can practice them now. Again, say, "I need something to eat" in each of those three tones.
>
> How did each tone feel to you? _____
>
> _____
>
> _____
>
> When you ask someone for something that you need, what tone do you think they will want to respond to? _____

Part 3: The words you use can also have an impact. Do you use respectful words, like "please" or "I would appreciate it if…" or "It would mean a lot to me"?

What words would convey respect? _____

_____

_____

How can you clearly describe your need? _____

_____

_____

Consider the need you identified at the beginning of this section. Write down the words you would like to say to share this need.

_____

_____

_____

_____

Try saying it out loud now, practicing volume and tone, and imagine their response. Keep practicing until you sound kind and respectful.

for you to know

Trust is the ability to depend on someone. You know they will be there for you and are reliable. Trust is not given. It is earned. A person earns trust by showing up and being dependable so that you can rely on them, over and over again.

Damien has been friends with Trent since freshman year, when they met in math class. Since then, they have come to depend on each other and now work like a team. Damien helps Trent with his math homework and studying for math tests. Trent always does better on his math tests when Damien helps him study. Trent is good at English and helps Damien write papers.

At the end of one quarter, a big math test was coming. Damien promised to come over the night before the test to help Trent study. But then Damien got a call from his girlfriend, who wanted to go to the movies that night. Damien decided to go to the movies with his girlfriend and skip studying with Trent. Damien called Trent.

"I can't come study tonight because something came up."

Trent felt irritated and replied, "What came up? We've been planning to study together ever since we heard there was going to be a test."

Damien fessed up: "Carla asked me to go out tonight and I decided to go with her."

Trent was hurt by Damien's decision and, though he studied that night, he didn't do as well on the test. He depended on Damien and felt that Damien had let him down. The next time Damien offered to study with him, Trent decided he needed to be more independent.

"No thanks," Trent said.

Damien apologized and asked, "What can I do to fix our relationship?"

Trent thought about it. "You could earn back my trust by doing the opposite of what you did to lose my trust. To believe in you again, I need you to be dependable and responsible, to follow through on what you say you'll do."

After a month or two of Damien showing up and helping when he said he would, Trent felt his trust in Damien was restored. At the same time, Trent began independently applying the study skills he had learned from Damien over time. This way, his math scores wouldn't depend so much on his friend's help.

for you to do

Let's explore trust! The more you know about it, the better you will be at using it. When someone consistently meets your needs, trust develops, which allows you to be vulnerable. When you can be vulnerable and express your thoughts and feelings, finding acceptance and support, you can feel safe in the relationship. Think about the relationships you have that are trusting. How did the other person earn your trust? How much of your trust do they have?

We trust in many different areas. We trust someone *physically* to show up or bring us something. We trust someone with our *thoughts* when we share them and trust the other person to be respectful by listening. We trust someone with our *feelings* when we can express them and trust the other person to care about them and validate them.

In the following chart, identify the people you trust, record how they earned your trust, and then assign a percentage point to indicate how much you trust them.

Person you trust	How they earned your trust	How much do you trust them? Rate from 0% to 100%
Mom	Keeping me safe, meeting my needs for food, shelter, and clothing	100%
My best friend	Listening, solving problems, having fun, having my back at school	80%

Person you trust	How they earned your trust	How much do you trust them? Rate from 0% to 100%

Now think about the people who trust you. How did you earn their trust?

Person who trusts you	How did you earn their trust?
Dad	Being reliable, responsible, honest, dependable

Person who trusts you	How did you earn their trust?

Have you ever lost someone's trust? Did you earn their trust back? If so, how? Describe what you did and how long it took.

Person whose trust I lost (and how)	How I earned it back
My sister, when I made fun of her in front of our friends	By being kind to her for several months, whether we were with others or alone

Person whose trust I lost (and how)	How I earned it back

Finally, think about people who have lost your trust and how they earned it back. If people who have lost your trust have not been able to earn it back, consider what you are expecting them to do in order to earn back your trust. Also, look at the chart where you recorded how you earned back trust that you had lost. It might give you ideas for how others can earn back your trust.

Person who lost my trust (and how)	How they earned it back
My boyfriend when he told me he was at work but was actually out with friends	By being honest and telling me the real reason he didn't want to hang out

Person who lost my trust (and how)	How they earned it back

more to do

When Suzie first met Rosie, she did not trust her at all. She simply introduced herself, not volunteering any information other than her name, where she went to school, and her grade level. Suzie shared impersonal information because no trust had developed yet. As Suzie spent more time with Rosie, and felt more comfortable with her, Suzie started sharing her thoughts on topics that Rosie brought up. Rosie respected Suzie's thoughts and feelings. This encouraged Suzie to share more of her thoughts and feelings. Even when Rosie did not agree with Suzie, she still respected Suzie's opinions and thoughts. Trust built between them over time.

When you give your trust to someone who has not earned it or are too quick to give it away, you can end up hurt and betrayed. On the following timeline, fill in how others earn your trust over time. How might you share small parts of yourself with someone until you know you can trust them?

Here is an example of how Suzie checked whether Rosie is trustworthy. When Rosie earned more trust, Suzie could increase the percentage and open up a bit more.

Percentage of trust	A way I can check whether someone is trustworthy	Did they earn more trust?
0%	I don't share personal information	Yes
10%	I share smaller thoughts, like "I think this could be done a different way," and see if they are respectful of those thoughts	Yes
20%	When she asked, "How are you today?" I answered honestly and watched to see if she was respectful of my smaller feelings	Yes

Now fill out your own trust percentage chart. As you do, think about how you need to feel respected in order to open up to someone more.

Percentage of trust	A way I can check whether someone is trustworthy	Did they earn more trust?
0%		
10%		
20%		
30%		
40%		
50%		
60%		
70%		
80%		
90%		
100%		

for you to know

It's impossible to be truly vulnerable, and feel safe, without trust. Trust makes vulnerability possible. To be vulnerable is to share the deepest parts of yourself with another, with the hope of finding acceptance and validation.

Being vulnerable by sharing personal thoughts and feelings with just anyone is a risk because, if they don't care for you, it can result in a broken heart. Developing trust first removes the risk from vulnerability. You will know your heart is safe with someone because they have already shown that they care about you.

You can be confident in your vulnerability! Maybe you feel strongly about something happening at school and you want to share these thoughts with a friend. Or you may be having a hard day if your parents had a fight or your grandmother is sick, for example, so you want to share your sad feelings with someone. When you share a thought or a feeling with another and they see you, hear you, feel you, or express understanding, the sense of connection in your relationship strengthens. Developing trust with someone first, then being vulnerable in ways that allow them to truly see you, is a formula that protects and grows your heart.

It can feel hard to be vulnerable, especially if your heart has been hurt before. Taking another chance can feel risky…unless you follow the formula of building trust before sharing vulnerability. Within a safe relationship, sharing who you really are—what you think and feel—is powerful. When someone tells you that those thoughts and feelings are important, it validates you as a person.

You are important and so are your thoughts and feelings. You have value, so by sharing yourself, you are acknowledged. Someone recognizes your value, and this validates you. When another sees you, hears you, and appreciates you, it builds the emotional intimacy you have with that person. As you feel safe to share yourself more, they feel safe to share themselves more. Your attachment grows stronger.

for you to do

When you think about being vulnerable, what comes to mind? Perhaps you have been vulnerable in the past and you were invalidated or betrayed in ways that hurt. In the future, you can follow the formula to develop trust before being vulnerable. Then your heart will be safer. However, this does not mean that being vulnerable again will feel easy. Think about the past, the present, and the future as you answer the following questions about vulnerability.

Think of a time in the past when you were vulnerable. Write about how it worked out for you. Did you build trust first and then someone validated your thoughts and feelings? Did you feel betrayed and suffer pain in your heart as a result?

_____

_____

_____

Your past experiences can impact your willingness to be vulnerable now. Do you think it will feel hard? Will it be easy? Write about why.

_____

_____

_____

Consider your current relationships and how much vulnerability you experience within them. It likely depends on the person, so write down three names. Then record whether you are able to be very vulnerable, somewhat vulnerable, or not vulnerable at all.

Person: _____ Vulnerability level: _____

Person: _____ Vulnerability level: _____

Person: _____ Vulnerability level: _____

Think about what impacts your vulnerability level. Do you feel your current relationships are not safe places to share? Maybe your relationships are safe, but you still struggle to feel safe enough to be vulnerable. Write down your thoughts and feelings about vulnerability.

_____

_____

_____

Moving forward, what would help you to be more vulnerable in your relationships? Maybe developing more trust first will help your heart feel safe. Or you could start new relationships with more trustworthy people. Write down some ideas.

_____

_____

_____

more to do

When you are vulnerable, you share thoughts and feelings. There may be parts of you that you have not shared with others, including family and friends. What are some thoughts and feelings that you have not shared, but would like to be able to share with someone?

Fill the thought bubbles with thoughts you would like to share.

Then fill the hearts with feelings you would like to share.

Now think of one person to share one heart or thought bubble with and write down their name.

_____

Has this person earned your trust? Circle one: Yes   No

Does your heart feel safe with them? Circle one: Yes   No

If the answer is yes, then go ahead. Share that thought or feeling with them this week! Afterward, write down their response.

_____

_____

_____

_____

for you to know

Healthy attachment is the foundation of good mental health. When you feel connected to others in healthy relationships, you experience an increase in self-esteem, a decrease in symptoms of anxiety and depression, and a sense of stability from having people to solve problems with and support you.

Mandy feels alone, even when she is surrounded by others. She has friends and talks to people. She sits with them at lunch or walks home from school with them. They talk about their favorite shows and music, who is dating who this week, and even their grades on a history test. But they don't know her. Mandy has never shared how she really feels with her friends. None of them know her parents are divorcing or that her older brother is struggling with substance abuse. She hasn't shared her thoughts about what she wants to do after high school and who she wants to be. She is never alone, yet feels so very unknown.

Mandy is learning about how attunement and trust lead to closer relationships. She sees that when there is a snack ready for her when she gets home from school, her mother knows her needs and is meeting them. This communicates to Mandy that she is important and has value. She sees that when her parents give her money for new shoes, they also know her need and are meeting it. Again, she feels cared for and valued. This is attunement and how Mandy can know who to trust. Mandy sees that her best friend always asks Mandy if she needs to talk at just the right time. It's like her friend knows Mandy so well, she can read Mandy's face and body language to know when Mandy is upset about something. Mandy's friend is attuned to her, "in tune" with her. Mandy can trust her friend and feel close enough to share vulnerable, personal thoughts and feelings. Mandy feels safe and secure in this relationship. As Mandy learns about growing her relationships with these steps, she feels more confidence in who she is.

for you to do

Think about a relationship you've had for a long time. Maybe with your parents, siblings, or a best friend. Using the following chart, think about how you built that relationship together. Write an example of how that person is attuned to you, an example of how you trust that person, an example of how you are able to be vulnerable with them, and an example of how you show attachment in your relationship. You likely have several attachment-based relationships, but never thought about them this way before. To fill this out for more relationships, download a copy of this chart at http://www .newharbinger.com/48725.

My important relationship: My Father

Attunement	He has rules that keep me safe
Trust	He keeps things I tell him between us
Vulnerability	When I share my feelings, he tries to understand them
Attachment	I feel safe with him so I ask him for help with solving problems

My important relationship: _____

Attunement	
Trust	
Vulnerability	
Attachment	

more to do

Attachment, or connection, with other people is all around you! Sometimes when you are not looking for something, you don't see it. However, when you look, you see it everywhere. This week look around at the relationships you see. Notice when you see people meeting each other's needs. Notice people who are trusting each other. Notice how attachment grows in family relationships and friendships. Then answer the following questions.

What relationship did you see *attuned* this week? Then describe how people were attuned to each other. What needs were they meeting for each other?

Relationship: _____

How I knew they were attuned: _____

_____

Needs they were meeting for each other: _____

_____

Did you see people trusting each other this week? How did you know they were trusting? Give a few examples.

_____

_____

_____

What did you notice about attachment in your own relationships this week?

_____

_____

_____

Is there attunement in your relationships?

_____

_____

_____

Is there trust in your relationships?

_____

_____

_____

How did you feel about what you noticed in your own relationships?

_____

_____

_____

Is it what you expected? In what ways? In what ways was it not what you expected?

_____

_____

_____

PART THREE

From Anxious to Secure Attachment

11 what you bring to a relationship

for you to know

Every person has talents, abilities, and strengths. You bring these into your relationships, offering them to the other person. By recognizing your talents, abilities, and strengths, and how you bring them into relationships, your self-confidence and social success will grow!

Rhonda knows what she does not do well. She has critical people in her life: a grandparent and a friend. They point out all the mistakes she makes and all the things she cannot do. She is not a good dancer, singer, or artist like her friend. She struggles with reading and writing, but her grandfather expects her to be a perfect student. After hearing so much about her weaknesses, she is focused on them. She has lost sight of things she can do well.

When Rhonda spoke to her mother about these frustrations, her mother reminded her of the things that Rhonda was good at: math, helping others, and training animals. Her mother helped Rhonda see that she did not need to be like anyone else or be who anyone else wanted her to be. She could be herself!

Think of the human body. Each part has a purpose. Some parts have a big job and some have a smaller role. The big parts can't do their job without the contribution of the smaller parts. The eye is small, but it has a big job because it steers the body. The eye tells the hands and feet where to move. If the eye said, "I want to be a hand because it is more important; it is better because it can pick things up," you'd have problems. If the eye was jealous of what the hand could do, and decided to stop seeing because it could not be a hand, you would have a body that wouldn't work the same way anymore.

Similarly, in every relationship, you have a job to do. You have talents, skills, abilities, and strengths that nobody else has in the same combination. That's what makes you uniquely you! Each relationship is unique through the comingling of two people's strengths and weaknesses. Attunement and meeting each other's needs are made possible by using your own strengths. Knowing what you have to contribute to a relationship can increase your confidence and decrease anxiety. In relationships, you

72

contribute strengths and abilities in ways that make the relationship better. You help someone else. In the same way, someone else uses their strengths and abilities in ways that help you and make the relationship better. We are stronger together!

for you to do

You have strengths and talents, things you bring to a relationship! Look at this list of strengths and abilities. Circle the ones that describe you. You can also ask a parent or friend to look at the list too. Sometimes others see your strengths more clearly than you do. They can help you recognize your abilities. You can download a copy of this list to print for them at http://www.newharbinger.com/48725.

Artistic	Athletic	Musical	Cooking	Writing	Intelligent
Wisdom	Courage	Analytical	Patience	Discipline	Languages
Technology	Friendly	Planner	Flexible	Team player	Communicative
Curiosity	Fair	Positivity	Humility	Kind	Good judgment
Leader	Spiritual	Funny	Hospitality	Studious	Imaginative
Reasonable	Investigative	Confident	Genuine	Sensitive	Inspiring

For each ability you circled, complete the following sentence.

My strength _Planner_ *can help me in relationships by* _planning activities with my friends_

73

My strength _____ can help me in relationships by _____

_____

My strength _____ can help me in relationships by _____

_____

My strength _____ can help me in relationships by _____

_____

My strength _____ can help me in relationships by _____

_____

My strength _____ can help me in relationships by _____

_____

more to do

Come up with a plan for how you can use your strengths this week. Having strengths and knowing what they are is the first step. The next step is to intentionally use them in your relationships! The best intention is nothing if not followed with a plan to make the intention become reality. Use the following formula to make a plan for this week. To plan for future weeks, download the formula at http://www.newharbinger.com/48725.

The strength I will use this week is: _____

This is *when* I will use it: _____

This is *where* I will use it: _____

This is *how* I will use it: _____

Now that you know which strength you want to use this week, fill in the following chart to measure your success!

My strength: _____			
	This is *when* I used it	This is *where* I used it	This is *how* I used it
Monday			
Tuesday			
Wednesday			
Thursday			
Friday			
Saturday			
Sunday			

12 boundaries in relationships

for you to know

An important part of relationships is knowing the *boundary* where you end and others begin. Having boundaries is like having a fence that helps you and others feel safe and secure.

Kirk always feels safe with Uncle Ted. Uncle Ted asks Kirk about his day and then actually listens to the answer. He asks questions to learn more. Kirk likes talking to Uncle Ted about things that are important to him.

During lunch one day, Kirk asked his uncle for advice about a friend who had betrayed him. Kirk described a few situations where his friend, Scott, pushed Kirk to do things he was not comfortable doing. Scott also let Kirk down several times when they were planning to hang out. Uncle Ted recommended more distance from Scott because he was not a trustworthy friend.

You need boundaries, or fences, that protect you. These fences keep people who are not trustworthy or respectful further from you. They also allow people you feel safe with to come closer. You decide where to set these boundaries based on the behaviors and choices of the people in your life. Boundaries can be emotional or physical. If someone close to you betrays you, you may push them back a little...or a lot. On the other hand, maybe a friend really showed up for you and was there when you needed them. You may open the gate in your fence to let them come closer, because you trust them. In a dating relationship, your physical boundaries may change as you get to know a person better, feel safer, and become more comfortable with them.

Your boundaries are not exactly like any another person's boundaries. This is because boundaries are based on your life experiences and no two people have the same life experiences. Some people's boundaries are further out. Others are set closer. Each person gets to decide where their boundaries are. You have control over your boundaries, and every person you meet has control over theirs.

When you respect another person's boundaries, it helps them feel safe with you. Relationships that feel safe are healthy. When you do not respect another person's boundaries by pushing them to do things that they say make them feel uncomfortable, this impacts the relationship. They may not want you to come closer to them or enter their personal space.

In the same way, you need to let people know what you want, and do not want, in a relationship. If someone does not respect your boundaries, you will not feel safe allowing them to come closer physically or emotionally. Respecting each other's boundaries is a great way to earn trust! Trust leads to deeper, healthier relationships.

for you to do

Think about your boundaries, where they are, and how you want to set them physically and emotionally. Consider the following questions about which people you allow inside your fence and who you keep outside your fence.

Write down how you set your physical fence. What boundaries do you have about physical contact with others? What is okay and what is not okay?

_____

_____

_____

Write about your emotional fences. What boundaries do you have about sharing emotions with others? Who do you share your feelings with and who do you keep at a distance?

_____

_____

_____

Write about the mental boundaries you have. What boundaries will help you know who to share your thoughts with?

_____

_____

_____

These questions explored three separate boundaries. Now, for each fence, identify who you want to let through the gate and who needs to stay outside the fence. Explore why.

Physical fence: _____

_____

Emotional fence: _____

_____

Mental fence: _____

_____

more to do

Part of having boundaries is knowing where yours are. Now think about the boundaries set by the people around you. It's also important to know where others have their boundaries. This week observe two friends or family members and notice where their boundaries are. Fill in the following chart to get to know your loved one's fences.

Boundaries	Loved one's name:	Loved one's name:
Physical		
Emotional		
Mental		

13 balance in relationships

for you to know

Trying to control another person, situation, or anything else that you do not actually have control over drives other people away. Control destroys relationships. If someone has ever tried to control you, you probably understand this. You only control yourself, as you are responsible for you. With this in mind, your relationships can be more balanced.

Howie promised he would pick Tom up from work because Tom's car was at the mechanic and his parents were out of town. When Howie didn't show up, Tom called other friends frantically until he found someone who could pick him up. At school the next day, Howie apologized and said he had fallen asleep.

From then on, anytime they were planning to get together, Tom asked repeatedly if Howie was going to show up. Tom called Howie an hour before they were meeting to remind him and confirm that he was coming. This went on for several weeks, and Howie started to feel upset that Tom was always checking on him. Howie understood that he had made a mistake and needed to earn Tom's trust back by showing up and being reliable. But he felt Tom wasn't giving him the chance to show that he was trustworthy.

Respecting the space and time of others, their thoughts and feelings, and their choices are all healthy ways to increase the strength of a relationship. Managing your anxious feelings, on your own, creates this space for others. It also allows the other person to feel valued. When you are trying to control someone else, it means you do not trust them. Your relationships will grow when you allow the space for trust to be earned, or earned back. The confidence you feel in secure attachment decreases anxiety. Then you can have confidence that your relationships will lead to healthy connections based in trust.

for you to do

Think about what causes you to experience anxiety in relationships. Is it fearing the relationship will not last? Are you scared about being alone? Do you worry that conflict leads to distance in relationships? Maybe you're concerned that you may not have value in the relationship. In the following chart, fill in the parts of a relationship that cause you anxiety. Then think about activities you can do that are calming and take care of your anxious feelings.

Things that cause me to feel anxious	How I can calm my anxiety
The thought of losing the relationship	Take a walk when I begin to worry

Things that cause me to feel anxious	How I can calm my anxiety

more to do

Trying to control things is a symptom of anxiety. When you feel worried, you may look for things you can control. You are trying to increase the chances that outcomes will turn out the way you want. However, relationships involve another person, and they have the freedom to make their own choices and have their own thoughts, feelings, and behaviors.

Using the following chart, think through a relationship that is important to you. Then make lists of the things that you can and cannot control about the relationship. To do this for multiple relationships, download a copy of this chart at http://www. newharbinger.com/48725.

Remember that you cannot control other people, so everything involving the other person should go in that column. You do have complete control over yourself, so everything that involves you should go in that column. In fact, no one controls you—just like you do not control someone else! Here's how Tom filled out the chart.

My important relationship: My best friend, Howie

I *can* **control**	I *cannot* **control**
Whether I choose to trust Howie again	Howie stood me up
Letting Howie earn my trust back	The risk that Howie might stand me up again
How I respond if Howie lets me down again	Howie being a trustworthy person

My important relationship: _____

I *can* control	I *cannot* control

Look at what you have listed. You may not be able to control how the other person chooses to act, but you do control your reactions to their choices and behaviors. When things about the relationship that you do not control start to upset or worry you, use calming activities to take care of your feelings: taking a walk, watching a favorite movie to distract yourself, asking a parent if you can help make dinner, playing your favorite song and singing along. These calming activities can help you take care of your feelings about not being in control. Your relationship may grow stronger as a result!

14 recognizing a good relationship

for you to know

A healthy relationship has mutual respect and understanding, give and take, balance. Recognizing that you have a relationship with these ingredients can calm your anxious feelings. By noticing good things, worry decreases.

Samantha likes being friends with Tabitha. But at times, Tabitha can overwhelm her. Once Tabitha invited Samantha for a sleepover, then kept asking her to stay another night. Samantha spent the whole weekend at Tabitha's house and didn't finish any homework. When she tried to leave, Tabitha got upset and said she just wanted to spend more time together. Samantha suspected Tabitha didn't like to be alone. Tabitha's parents both worked long hours and she had no siblings. She was often home alone and hated being by herself. She felt lonely, so she clung to Samantha. When Tabitha asked Samantha for help with homework, Samantha suspected that her friend could actually do it on her own. She asked Tabitha about it and Tabitha admitted that she liked having help because she didn't feel confident doing it alone.

There's nothing wrong with needing help on an assignment! However, when you actually know the concepts and are asking for help because of a lack of confidence, there is another solution. Boost your confidence! When you don't feel confident about completing tasks on your own, your anxiety shows up in the relationships you are depending on too much.

Anxiety can also arise when your needs are not being consistently met. You may then cling to anyone who does meet your needs because you aren't sure when your needs will be met again. Grow trust in your relationships through witnessing your friends being reliable and dependable in physical and emotional ways. This will show you that your needs will be met consistently. Giving your friends the time and space to earn your trust, as you patiently observe their consistency, can build strong relationships that are secure and safe for you.

for you to do

You probably have healthy relationships. But it can feel hard to recognize them because of the anxiety you feel in relationships. When you know what to look for, and can recognize healthy aspects of your relationships, you can calm your anxiety. By realizing that your relationship needs are met, you no longer have to worry about the inconsistency you experienced in the past.

Look at the traits listed in the following chart and think about whether they are present in any of your current relationships. Choose two relationships, perhaps a family member and a friend, and use this chart to compare and contrast those relationships. If a healthy relationship trait applies, put a checkmark in the box.

Relationship traits	Friend's name:	Family member's name:
They listen to me when I talk about things that are important to me		
I feel seen		
I feel heard		
My emotions matter to them		
My thoughts are respected		
They make time for me		
They respect me		
I feel valued by them		
They care about my needs		

If you find that most of these traits are present in one or both of those relationships, then it is a healthy relationship—you can rest and relax knowing your needs will be consistently met. If some of these traits are missing in your relationships, then those traits are the ones to practice and develop.

more to do

As you look at the relationship traits and recognize that they are healthy characteristics, you can start looking for these traits in future relationships. Finding them will increase the health and security of your attachments. Answer these questions to consider your beliefs about relationships.

Is it possible for you to have a relationship that includes the things in the list of healthy traits? Why or why not? Have you seen or experienced this type of relationship before?

_____

_____

_____

_____

What would it mean to you to have a relationship with these traits? Would you be able to rest and relax in that relationship? Why or why not?

_____

_____

_____

_____

Even if a relationship meets your needs consistently, if relationships in the past have not, you may expect that your needs won't be met. Based on past experiences, you may still have anxiety in your relationships. Managing that anxiety will help your relationships be more secure. How can you manage your feelings of anxiety in relationships?

Look at this list and choose three calming activities to try this week when you feel anxious about your relationships. Calming your emotions will help you reduce the amount of anxiety you express in your relationships. This will bring stability to your attachments.

Take a walk outside	Watch a funny video	Listen to your favorite song
Call a friend	Do a craft	Watch your favorite movie
Draw	Put lotion on	Do yoga

PART FOUR

From Avoidant to Secure Attachment

15 no one is perfect

for you to know

Forgiveness is not for the other person, it's for *you*! Forgiveness frees you and allows you to move forward. Not forgiving people leads to bitterness and continued pain that can affect other relationships because you don't want to get hurt again.

Most people try to avoid hurting others, but no one is perfect. Everyone makes mistakes and even hurts others. Hurtful words are said, actions lead to hurt feelings, respect may not be used, and irresponsible behaviors can let you down. When those things happen, apologies can heal relationships and move everyone toward restoration. If someone apologizes, but the other person does not forgive, the relationship will not be reconciled. Forgiveness happens when you accept the apology. Then restoration becomes possible. The equation is: *Apology + Forgiveness = Restoration*.

In the restoration phase, you can decide whether to give the other person another chance. This does not mean that your original hurt is erased or repaired. It takes time to reestablish trust, which happens when the person who hurt you uses attunement to show they care. When trust has been lost, people must earn it back in the same way it was originally earned.

However, sometimes the other person is not sorry and does not ask for forgiveness. If that happens, it is painful. But you can still forgive them to release yourself from feelings of pain and resentment. The relationship may not be restored, sadly, but you will be free of the negative feelings that could prevent you from engaging in other relationships.

Caryn has two friends who hurt her. Steph betrayed her trust when she told someone else one of Caryn's secrets. Caryn felt embarrassed and angry, but Steph apologized. Caryn felt her friend was sincere and forgave her. Caryn decided to give Steph a chance to earn her trust back. While she withheld her most private thoughts for a while, over time she opened up to share more with Steph.

Her other friend, Jan, began secretly dating Caryn's boyfriend. When Caryn found out, she was angry and sad. Her boyfriend left her for Jan. While Jan said she was sorry, she did not change her behavior and continued to date Caryn's ex-boyfriend. Caryn decided not to give Jan another chance. She eventually forgave Jan for the betrayal, but Jan did not try to rebuild trust and Caryn also did not give her the opportunity. Their relationship ended.

for you to do

In relationships, ruptures or breaks happen. Others will make mistakes or let you down, and you will feel disappointed by their words and choices. Think about a time when a friend said or did something hurtful. Then answer these questions.

What happened that was hurtful?

_____

_____

_____

Did the person apologize? How did they respond to your hurt? Did that response help heal the relationship?

_____

_____

_____

Did you forgive them? What did you decide about continuing a relationship with them?

_____

_____

_____

Did they earn your trust back? If yes, what did they do or say that showed trustworthiness? Are you willing to feel vulnerable with them again?

_____

_____

_____

_____

How has this event changed your relationship?

_____

_____

_____

_____

more to do

When you extend forgiveness to another, it's good to remember that forgiveness has been extended to you too. You have made mistakes in relationships, as no one is perfect. The grace extended to you when others forgave you is the same grace that you pass on to others. Think about a time when you hurt someone and said or did something that caused a rupture in your relationship. Then answer the following questions.

What were the actions or words that someone else found hurtful?

_____

_____

_____

Did you apologize? If so, was it healing for the relationship? What did you do to show that your apology was sincere?

_____

_____

_____

Did the other person forgive you? Did they choose to continue the relationship?

_____

_____

_____

How did you earn their trust back? Are you both willing to be vulnerable with each other once again?

_____

_____

_____

How has the event changed your relationship?

_____

_____

_____

16 relationship rupture and repair

for you to know

Disagreements are expected in relationships. When disagreements are not handled fairly, ruptures between people can happen. When a rupture happens, repair must follow—or else the relationship can become distanced and disconnected.

When two people have conversations, there will be disagreements. Every person has their own thinking process, perspective, and worldview. Everyone is entitled to their opinions, thoughts, and feelings. These rarely match the opinions, thoughts, and feelings of another person perfectly. When you don't see things the same way as another person, a disagreement happens. This is not a problem in itself. What matters is *how* you handle it. When you approach the disagreement with fairness, you can avoid a relationship rupture.

for you to do

Using the following chart, identify the rules of fair fighting you already use and those you need to work on more. Place a checkmark in the column that applies for each statement.

Principles of fair disagreements	I use this consistently	I need to work on this
I use a calm tone of voice		
I do not yell		
I listen without interrupting		
I ask for a break when I am getting upset		
I do not call people names or curse		
I stay focused on the current topic		
I express my concerns clearly using my words		
I talk about my own thoughts and feelings		
I don't blame people, and instead look for solutions		
I am willing to compromise in ways that help us settle the disagreement		
During discussions, I use respect, find equality, and seek balance		
I use kind words		

Keep these principles of fair disagreement in mind. During a disagreement, they can help you avoid a relationship rupture. Practice the principles, especially if you checked the "I need to work on this" column.

more to do

If a rupture has occurred, repairing it is important to reestablish connection. During a rupture, a relationship no longer feels emotionally safe and secure. You have not applied fair disagreement principles, so an apology can repair the relationship.

During a disagreement, if you called someone a name, became angry and yelled, did not listen and instead spoke over someone, or discredited their thoughts or feelings, the way to repair the disconnection in the relationship is to apologize. Apologizing is a social skill you can use to take responsibility for your choices and actions, repair the rupture, and commit to work on changing behaviors that hurt someone.

When both people got upset and were yelling or being disrespectful, then apologies from both people can help heal the relationship. Because you can only control yourself, not the other person, you are only responsible for your apology. They need to make their own decision about apologizing. If they choose not to, your feelings about the relationship may be impacted as you decide whether or not you can feel safe with this person.

To keep a relationship healthy, repairing ruptures is necessary. Recall two arguments or disagreements you had in the past and write down the names of the people involved. Consider the following questions and write the answers in the chart.

Repairing ruptures	Past disagreement with:	Past disagreement with:
What did we argue about?		
Was I arguing fairly during the disagreement?		
Were they arguing fairly during the disagreement?		
How did the argument end: In a compromise? In a rupture?		
Does this relationship feel disconnected as a result of the disagreement?		
Was the relationship repaired, perhaps with an apology?		
Would fair fighting and relationship repair have changed the outcome?		

17 interdependence and you

for you to know

We need each other. A balance between dependence and independence results in *interdependence*. By meeting each other's needs, mutually, you can have a healthy relationship. Here are three stories that show the differences and similarities between dependence, independence, and interdependence.

Dependence: Ty and Devon have known each other for years. Devon has always felt responsible for Ty because Ty has a hard time speaking up for himself, defending himself, and organizing his homework. Devon protects Ty from bullies, invites Ty to join him and his friends in activities, reminds Ty when assignments are due, and offers to help Ty complete the work. Ty appreciates Devon's help and constantly thanks him for the support. Ty knows he depends heavily on Devon and thinks he should be more independent, but it's comfortable to allow Devon to take care of him. Their relationship has become enmeshed, where one person needs the other, and is out of balance.

Independence: Ty and Devon are friends who enjoy spending time together. They each have things that are important to them. Ty likes to play sports and will often go to practices after school. Devon has a job that he works on weekends and a few weekday afternoons. They see each other after they have each completed their homework, when time allows, so they don't get together that often. They keep in touch on social media and have lunch together a few times a week when their class schedules coincide. They are completely separate people who do not need each other and are entirely independent from each other.

Interdependence: Ty and Devon are best friends who have known each other since kindergarten. They are different people, but enjoy spending time together, and supporting each other. Ty plays sports and Devon attends the games, when his work schedule permits, to cheer Ty on. When Devon is working, Ty often drops by to bring him coffee or check in about how things are going. They get together a few times a week to help each other with homework, because Ty is good at math and science, and Devon is good at English and history. They each use their strengths to help the other, providing support in a give-and-take relationship. Attunement is present and trust has grown!

for you to do

When you have been independent for a long time, taking care of yourself and meeting all your own needs, it can feel strange to become interdependent. You need to start looking for others' needs in order to meet them. You can also be vulnerable to let others see your needs, and then be accepting when they meet those needs.

Read the following scenarios and identify whether they are *dependent*, *independent*, or *interdependent*. The answer code is at the end of this activity.

1. Carl is stuck on a homework assignment and calls his friend Mark for help.

   _____

2. Nance is having a hard day. When her friend notices, she suggests that they have lunch together so they can talk. Nance agrees.

   _____

3. Marc calls his sister to ask for a ride home from work. Later that night, their mother asks Marc if he used the money she gave him to catch a cab home from work. His sister is agitated.

   _____

4. Liam misses an important job interview because his car has a flat tire and he doesn't want to inconvenience anyone by asking for help.

   _____

5. Karin quickly leaves class in tears about her boyfriend. Her friends negotiate who should follow her to give support since this has become a daily occurrence.

   _____

6. Neveah struggles with tests but studying is hard for her. She chooses to study alone because she doesn't want her friends to know how hard it is.

   _____

more to do

Interdependence feels satisfying in a relationship. Each person gives and takes, mutually and equally, to create balance. When one person is always taking and not giving, it can stress a relationship. In the same way, if each person is wholly taking care of themselves, then their focus is on themselves and their own needs. This blocks the development of attunement, trust, and vulnerability. Instead, when each person is focused on the other person and meeting their needs, then all needs are met within intimacy and connection. This strengthens the relationship. Think about the following questions and what meaning each relationship style has for you.

When you think about a dependent relationship, what comes to mind? What are your beliefs about dependence? Is it ever appropriate? How does this type of relationship feel to you?

_____

_____

_____

When you think about an independent relationship, what comes to mind? What are your beliefs about independence? Is it ever appropriate? How does this type of relationship feel to you?

_____

_____

_____

When you think about an interdependent relationship, what comes to mind? What are your beliefs about interdependence? Is it ever inappropriate? How does this type of relationship feel to you?

_____

_____

_____

Answer Key

1. Interdependence

2. Interdependence

3. Dependence

4. Independence

5. Dependence

6. Independence

18 compromise in relationships

for you to know

Compromise happens when you listen to the wishes of another person, they listen to your wishes, and then you both meet in the middle. Everyone gets some of what they want, but probably not all of what they want.

Jayme and Mark were trying to decide how to spend their afternoon. Jayme really wanted to see a new movie and Mark wanted to practice basketball for an upcoming game. Jayme listened while Mark explained why it was important to practice for the game.

"My team depends on me. In our last game, I feel like I really let them down on a free throw. I need to practice so I can earn their respect back and help win the game."

Jayme reframed what he heard Mark say, to show he was listening and understood what his friend was saying. "I hear you saying that you need to practice so your team can depend on you in the next game, because you feel like you let them down during the last game. I understand why that's important to you."

Then Mark listened as Jayme explained why it was important to see the movie. "You know I've been so excited about this movie. I saw the trailer last summer and have been waiting for it to come out. My parents said they will take me, but I really want to see it with you because we saw the first three movies in the series together and you get it. My parents are being nice to take me, but they don't get this series like you do!"

Mark repeated what he heard Jayme say to confirm that he heard his friend. "You don't want to see the movie with someone else; you want to see it with me. We've seen the other ones together and it's only right for us to see this one together too. I agree! I look forward to watching that movie with you too!"

Then they thought about the needs present, because needs must be met before wants. While practicing for Mark's game was not a physical need that would keep him alive, it was a need when it came to his character and reputation among his team. It met his need for acceptance. So they compromised.

Jayme said, "Let's practice basketball today so you feel ready and confident for the game."

"Then next weekend after the game, instead of going out with the team, we'll go to the movie to celebrate," Mark suggested.

"It will be tough, "Jayme said with a smile, "but I'll be patient and not see the movie before then."

for you to do

When one person always gets what they want in a relationship and insists on having everything their way, it feels uncomfortable to the other person. Finding balance is realizing that no one has needs or wants that are more important than the needs and wants of another person. This brings equality and respect. In relationships, attunement is the foundation for building feelings of safety and attachment. Part of feeling loved and valued is filling the need to be heard and understood. Your thoughts and feelings are important, and so are the thoughts and feelings of your friends. Think about the importance of compromise in relationships as you answer the following questions. Consider your current relationships and the role compromise plays in them.

How do you use compromise now? In the last week, did you use this skill?

_____

_____

_____

_____

What is the hardest part of compromising? Maybe it's listening to another, expressing your own needs and wants, or finding the common ground in the middle.

_____

_____

_____

_____

How would using compromise improve your relationships?

_____

_____

_____

_____

How might others react to your use of compromise? How would they feel about compromising with you?

_____

_____

_____

_____

How would you feel about your relationships if they involved more compromise?

_____

_____

_____

_____

Are you able to delay satisfying your wants to meet someone else's needs? Why or why not?

_____

_____

_____

_____

Do you want to have everything your way? Or are you able to give up some things you want to allow someone else to have some things they want? How might this choice impact your relationships?

_____

_____

_____

_____

more to do

This week, when you need to compromise with a friend, use this chart to explore the needs and wants in the situation. Doing so will help you find a good compromise. During the conversation, take a break to complete this form. Record the important points for each person, then resume the discussion. For future compromises with friends, download a copy of this chart at http://www.newharbinger.com/48725.

Questions for a compromise	Me	My friend:
What do we each need?		
Is one need more urgent than the other?		
Is there a way that both needs can be met? If not, write "no." If yes, write down ideas.		
What do we each want?		

Is there a way that both wants can be met? If not, write "no." If yes, write down ideas.		
What could the compromise be?		
What would each person get from the compromise?		
What would each person give up with the compromise?		

You can use a chart like this over and over again, each time you need to practice compromise. The more you use compromise, the more it will come naturally. Your relationships will benefit.

PART FIVE

From Disorganized to Secure Attachment

19 control your emotions so they don't control you

for you to know

Managing your emotions is your responsibility. When your emotions are in control of you, you may not make the best choices. You may become angry at a friend over something that could have been managed, thereby damaging the relationship. If no one showed you how to take care of your feelings, rather than hoping other people will take care of them, you are likely controlled by your emotions. This can hurt relationships until you learn how to control your own emotions. Taking a few deep breaths to regain control of your emotions can lead to clearer thinking and decision making. When you take responsibility for how you feel, you can have healthier relationships.

Kara is a likeable girl who is on the cheerleading team, gets decent grades, and has cool parents who don't mind lots of Kara's friends hanging out at the house on weekends. She makes friends easily and always has a group of people around her. She has a hard time keeping friends, however, because Kara gets very angry. When someone does something she doesn't like, or touches her things, or says something that feels unkind to her, Kara explodes with anger. She yells, screams, curses, and often throws things.

This doesn't happen once in a while; it happens every day. There is always something upsetting Kara, so friends quickly grow tired of dealing with her anger and start avoiding her. Because they don't feel safe with Kara, they can't trust her. As a result, Kara is always looking for new friends. She wonders why no one wants to spend time with her, and no one is brave enough to tell her the real reason. She doesn't understand that her anger scares people.

When you are experiencing strong emotions, like anger, you might want others to calm you down, make you feel better, and help you take care of your feelings. But friends grow tired of continuously calming you down and helping you to regain control of, or regulate, your emotions. Everyone is responsible for their own emotions. We need to be able to calm ourselves down, not depending on others to take care of us. Emotions that are out of control make it hard for others to feel close to us. Like Kara, maybe you don't like feeling all alone with your feelings. You need to understand your feelings better and learn how to care for them so that they don't impact your relationships in a negative way.

There are three steps to learning how to care for, control, and regulate your emotions. The first step is to know what your emotions are.

for you to do

Relationships tend to bring out big emotions in us. Here are some descriptions of emotions. Think about the last time you experienced each one within a relationship. Perhaps a friend or family member brings out the most emotion in you. Consider that relationship as you answer the following questions.

Happy is feeling good, light, and bright when something good happens. *The last time I felt happy was when* _____

_____

Sad is feeling low, down, and "blue" when something hurts. *The last time I felt sad was when* _____

_____

Fear is feeling scared, nervous, and frightened when something feels dangerous. *The last time I felt fear was when* _____

_____

Anger is feeling mad, rageful, and explosive when something upsets you. *The last time I felt anger was when* _____

_____

Frustrated is when something feels hard and you have to keep trying. *The last time I felt frustrated was when* _____

_____

Disappointed is when you look forward to something, but then it doesn't happen. *The last time I felt disappointed was when* _____

_____

Now that you can see your emotions more clearly, and observe when you tend to feel them, the next step is learning how to express them appropriately. Look at the emotions listed in the following chart. Consider the safe ways that you can express them, then answer the questions.

Emotion	Safe expression	Unsafe expression
Happy	Smiling, high fiving	Jumping on a desk
Sad	Crying, being quiet	Hurting yourself or others
Fear	Leaving a situation, saying, "I'm afraid"	Yelling and cursing
Anger	Punching a pillow, tearing up paper	Destroying anyone's property
Frustrated	Taking a break, deep breathing	Throwing things
Disappointed	Crying, saying, "I'm disappointed"	Blaming another person

What are emotions in the chart that you express safely?

_____

_____

What are emotions in the chart that you express unsafely?

_____

_____

Unsafe expressions are the ones you will want to work on. Try using the column of safe emotional expressions to start learning new ways of taking care of your feelings. This will help you learn to share emotions with others in healthy ways.

The last step is being able to cope by calming your emotions. Even happy emotions need to be calmed, because if you don't manage your happy feelings, they can have harmful results too. Many high school seniors have a hard time managing their happy feelings the week before graduation and make bad choices when they celebrate—with painful consequences. Here is a list of coping skills and strategies for each emotion.

Happy: keep a journal to write about your feelings, talk to a friend, scream into a pillow, dance

Sad: eat a spearmint candy, ask a loved one for a hug, have a snack or a drink of water

Fear: chew gum, count backward from 100, do jumping jacks, take a walk

Anger: take five deep breaths, eat a butterscotch candy, smell cologne or body spray on your wrist

Frustrated: tear apart cotton balls, bounce your leg, color or draw, listen to your favorite song

Disappointed: take a warm shower, watch an episode of your favorite show, do three yoga poses

more to do

It's important to know the coping skills that work for you before you actually need them. Everyone is different and each person has favorites. This week choose one coping skill for each emotion and try it out! After you have tried the coping skill, answer the following questions. To try more skills, download the questions at http://www .newharbinger.com/48725.

Which coping skill did you use for what feeling? _____

_____

How did you feel before you used the coping skill? _____

_____

Was the coping skill hard or easy to use? _____

_____

How did you feel after you used the coping skill? _____

_____

Will you use this coping skill again? Why or why not? _____

_____

for you to know

Empathy happens when you use your own emotions to connect with and understand the emotions of another. You don't need to share that person's experiences to understand their feelings. Connecting emotionally, through trust and vulnerability, deepens relationships.

Taylor has been friends with Monika for years. They do everything together and spend time hanging out every afternoon. When Taylor hears that Monika's mother has died, she doesn't know how to react. She understands her friend must be sad, but Taylor never lost a mother so she worries whether she can relate to Monika anymore. This makes Taylor very anxious. When she sees Monika at school, she starts avoiding her because Taylor doesn't know what to say. Their friendship grows more distant. Then Monika comes to visit Taylor one day after school.

"I miss our friendship," Monika tells Taylor.

"Maybe it's better if we aren't friends anymore," Taylor replies.

"Why? We've always been good friends."

Taylor gives Monika a sad look and says, "We don't have anything in common."

"Sure we do. We have all the same things in common that we used to. The only thing that changed is that my mom died," Monika said. "Wait! Is that what's wrong? You haven't been the same since my mom died."

"Yes!" Taylor exclaimed. "I don't know what to do. I don't know how to be your friend anymore. My mom didn't die, so I can't know how you feel. Wouldn't you like a friend who understands? Someone else who's been through what you've been through?"

"Taylor," Monika starts, "I don't need someone who's going through the same thing I am; I need my best friend. You know me better than anyone else. When I feel sad, you know how to make me laugh. When I feel scared, you know how to give me a hug and make me feel comfortable enough to talk about it. Those are the things I need right now. You can be my friend and do those things."

"But I don't know how you feel, so how can I help?" Taylor asks.

"I feel sad. And you know what sad feels like, right?" Monika replies. Taylor nods. "I feel helpless that I couldn't make my mother feel better or help her. But I know you felt helpless too, when your dad lost his job and you couldn't do anything to help. Our experiences might be different, but we all have the same feelings."

"I'm sorry, Monika," Taylor says. "I haven't been a very good friend. I promise to be better, to be the same old friend I've always been." Taylor smiles at Monika as they head into the kitchen to find a snack.

Knowing your own emotions helps you understand the emotions of others. You can recognize when another person is feeling sad, happy, mad, or scared by their body language, facial expressions, and words.

When you offer empathy to a friend, it communicates to them that they can trust you with their feelings and be emotionally vulnerable. They can share their emotions with you because you will recognize those emotions and know how to offer support to them.

for you to do

Not everyone expresses emotions in the same way, so watch a friend this week and observe how they show their emotions. By placing yourself in their shoes, thinking about what would help you, it can help you brainstorm what to offer your friend. For example, if when you feel sad it helps to have someone just sitting quietly with you, then when you see a friend feeling sad you can offer the same support.

In the following chart, identify what emotions look like, in yourself and in others. Then think about things that would help you to cope with that feeling. Those things could also help a friend when they are experiencing a similar emotion. This is the support that you can offer to them.

Emotions	Me	My friend:
Sad	My body language My shoulders slump, my arms cross	Their body language They fidget with their hands and their foot taps
	My facial expression My face is downcast, I cry	Their facial expression They have no light in their eyes, their eyebrows furrow
	My words "I don't want to talk"	Their words "I'm fine," when they're really not
	Supports that help me Someone sitting quietly with me	Supports I can offer them To talk or sit quietly together

Emotions	Me	My friend:
Sad	My body language	Their body language
	My facial expression	Their facial expression.
	My words	Their words
	Supports that help me	Supports I can offer them
Mad	My body language	Their body language
	My facial expression	Their facial expression
	My words	Their words
	Supports that help me	Supports I can offer them

Scared	My body language	Their body language
	My facial expression	Their facial expression
	My words	Their words
	Supports that help me	Supports I can offer
Happy	My body language	Their body language
	My facial expression	Their facial expression
	My words	Their words
	Supports that help me	Supports I can offer

more to do

Focus on the people around you to see if you can identify times when they are experiencing emotions you recognize. Answer the following questions as you apply empathy to your relationships.

Who did you observe this week (friends, family, others)?

_____

_____

What emotions did you recognize?

_____

_____

How did you identify the emotions (body language, facial expressions, words)?

_____

_____

When you recognized the emotions, what support did you offer?

_____

_____

How did people respond when you offered support?

_____

_____

How did you feel after you offered support?

_____

_____

reducing impulsivity and increasing self-control 21

for you to know

Having healthy relationships includes listening, staying in a conversation, and keeping an open mind—even if you do not like what is being said. You have self-control when you regulate yourself, stay open to other people's thoughts and feelings, and accept when they say no to something you want. You can be patient and put the concerns of others before your own.

Mica and Sarah were planning to spend Saturday hanging out. Sarah wanted to go hiking but Mica hates being outside, especially on a hot day. Mica was getting ready to say no, but changed her mind and decided to try hiking. She kept an open mind and was willing to try something that her friend liked. She enjoyed the beautiful views from hilltops, the times they sat to rest and chat, and the way her body felt strong and refreshed. These were payoffs for keeping an open mind. Best of all, she and Sarah got quality time together. Their friendship felt closer after doing something Sarah loved. At the end of the day, Mica was glad she went because she discovered she liked hiking and wanted to go again!

Jake wanted to borrow the family car to take the new girl in his economics class, Lana, to a concert. He asked his father, who said no because Jake's sister needed to take it to work. Jake started to get hot, his face flushed red, and his hands clenched. He felt his heart racing and knew he was getting ready to explode. He had been working up the nerve to ask this special girl out for weeks! But Jake also knew that if he exploded at his father, he would be grounded and it would be a month before he could use the family car. Jake used a technique to calm his anger. He took five deep breaths and walked out of the living room, continuing out the door and around the block. By the time he returned home, he was in a calmer state physically because he had moved his body and released the angry energy. He was also in a more peaceful state emotionally, as with that time to calm down he could consider possible alternatives. He asked his father if he could borrow the car on Saturday instead. His father said that sounded like a great plan. Jake texted Lana and she replied that she was free on Saturday. He got to take a special girl out, maintained a good relationship with his father, and averted a crisis—all by applying self-control.

for you to do

To increase self-control, apply the following techniques. Next to each one, write whether you think this will be an easy or difficult step, and why. Then practice these steps over the next week. The more you practice them, the easier they will become.

Techniques for self-control	Will it feel easy or difficult? Why?
When you feel impatient, worked up emotionally, or impulsive, these relaxation techniques can help. **Deep breathing:** Breathe in for a count of four, hold it for a count of four, then breathe out for a count of four. **Progressive muscle relaxation:** Lie down. Starting with your feet, tense and relax your muscles. Continue to tense and relax muscles up your body until you reach your face. Increase your self-awareness and, at the earliest sign of upset, use these calming skills to manage your feelings.	
Getting good sleep can help reduce reactivity. When you feel tired, you may have a harder time being patient and understanding. Teenagers need ten to twelve hours of sleep a night.	
Focus on the big picture instead of fixating on the present challenge. How will the decision you are making right now impact your future a year from now or five years from now? Set a goal and focus on achieving it instead of the smaller, possibly frustrating, steps to get there.	

When feeling impatient, emotional, or impulsive, **get some exercise.** Moving your body increases the flow of blood that can burn adrenaline, a hormone present when you get upset.	
Stop what you are doing to think. Make a list of the pros and cons about the thing you are feeling impatient about. Then consider whether the rewards are worth the inconvenience of waiting or coming up with alternative plans.	

more to do

When you are impatient in relationships, cannot accept someone saying no to you, or make decisions quickly without thinking about the consequences, your relationships can be negatively impacted. This makes it more difficult for others to feel close to you. People need to feel safe sharing their thoughts and feelings with you. When they feel safe, they are willing to be vulnerable and express their true selves.

Do your friends feel you will be patient when they are trying to change something about themselves or they want to share something that requires more of your time? Does your dating partner feel safe to say no if they aren't comfortable with something? In the following boxes, write your thoughts about key terms. For each term, describe it in your own words. Then write how this trait can impact your relationships, positively or negatively.

Key term: Patient

My definition	How it impacts my relationships

Key term: Self-control

My definition	How it impacts my relationships

Key term: Impulsive

My definition	How it impacts my relationships

for you to know

The "golden rule" is to treat others the way you want to be treated. It's a very healthy relationship rule! Following it helps others to feel safe in relationship with you, which builds secure attachments.

Kimmy has a hard time keeping friends. She likes for people to listen to her when she is talking, but she doesn't listen to others. She becomes angry when others interrupt her and are not listening to her because she wants people to respect her. But she is not respectful to them, and when upset, she curses at others and calls them names. If anyone calls her a name, Kimmy punishes them by ghosting them completely. Kimmy wants others to share their clothes and lunches with her. Yet she never shares and is possessive of her belongings. Kimmy does not treat others as she wants to be treated, which makes others uncomfortable around her. They have a hard time trusting her, so they don't want to risk being vulnerable with her. It's not long before they start avoiding her.

Jimmy is in Kimmy's class, and he has a tight circle of friends because he has a different attitude. In conversation, he talks and then listens to friends tell their side of the story. People like talking to Jimmy because he listens, and then offers good advice that is thoughtful. They trust Jimmy because he shows that he cares about them. It's easy for friends to be vulnerable and share their struggles. He likes to help his friends because he knows that whenever he has a hard time, it helps to talk it through with someone. Together, brainstorming solutions is more creative. Jimmy knows that since this is helpful for him, it's probably helpful for his friends also. He treats them the same way he wants to be treated. And it works! Because Jimmy listens and helps his friends, they do the same thing for him. His relationships are strong and close.

for you to do

Being kind to others because you want them to be kind to you is a great way to show respect and grow trust. Think about the types of relationships you want to have with friends, siblings, parents, and teachers. What would the perfect friend be like? In the following clouds, write some things that are important to you in a friend or other relationship.

What kinds of things would you do with each other (like play basketball or go to the movies)?

What type of person do you want to have a relationship with (maybe someone who is creative or adventurous)?

How would this person treat you (they'd listen to you and be respectful of your thoughts, feelings, and choices)?

more to do

Since you need to treat others the way you want to be treated, look at the things you identified as important to you in another person. To find that kind of friend or relationship, you need to be that kind of person too! Now you know what you must do, be the type of friend you want to have!

Those six things you wrote in the clouds may feel too big to accomplish. Sometimes a big goal can feel impossible. Here, break the larger goal into smaller goals. Take each of the six cloud descriptions and write one small task that you can do to move toward your goal. This is your starting place.

Cloud 1: _____

One small task: _____

Cloud 2: _____

One small task: _____

Cloud 3: _____

One small task: _____

Cloud 4: _____

One small task: _____

Cloud 5: _____

One small task: _____

Cloud 6: _____

One small task: _____

Now try to do one small task each day this week. Record what happens to your relationships. Do they start to grow?

_____

_____

_____

_____

_____

_____

_____

23 respect in relationships

for you to know

Respect happens when you view yourself as equal to other people, not more or less important. You may believe your thoughts, feelings, and opinions are more important. You may also think your thoughts, feelings, and opinions are less important. When you find the balance as equals, you will have relationships that mutually respect thoughts, feelings, and opinions.

Scenario 1: Brian and Sam have been friends for many years. Brian thinks he is more important than others and often demands they do things his way. He asserts that his thoughts are always right, that his feelings deserve everyone's attention, and that his opinions need agreement. Sam thinks he is less important than others, so when he is with Brian, he does everything the way Brian wants it done. Sam listens to Brian without ever disagreeing or voicing what he really thinks. Sam has his own thoughts, feelings, and opinions, but he keeps them to himself because he doesn't feel safe with Brian. Why share them if no one would be interested in them anyhow?

Scenario 2: Brian and Sam have a balanced view of respect and importance. They show their respect by listening to each other. When Brian is talking about something important to him, Sam listens and then presents his own thoughts about the topic. They have a discussion. If they don't agree, they agree to disagree because they respect each other's opinions. When Sam talks about his feelings, Brian accepts that this is how his friend feels and offers support. This relationship feels safe for Brian and Sam because they both find respect, acceptance, and support within it.

for you to do

A secure relationship provides a safe place where you can share thoughts and feelings, knowing that you will receive acceptance and support. Respect makes this type of a relationship possible. Think about two friendships you have, then ask yourself some questions to assess whether or not these relationships are characterized by respect. Place a checkmark in the box when the characteristic is present in that relationship.

Characteristics of respect	My friendship with:	My friendship with:
I accept their thoughts		
They accept my thoughts		
I accept their feelings		
They accept my feelings		
We agree to disagree		
I feel more important than them		
I feel less important than them		
I honor their wishes		
They honor my wishes		
I honor their rights		
They honor my rights		
I value their abilities		
They value my abilities		

more to do

Respect earns trust. It leads to vulnerability because relationships with respect are safe places. This week resolve to be respectful in the two friendships from the previous chart. Knowing information is a good first step, and the second step is applying it. This will bring change and increase the health of your relationships. Fill in the boxes with examples of how you showed respect this week.

Respectful actions	My friend's name:	My friend's name:
This week I practiced accepting their thoughts by listening and asking curious questions.	When Sam talked about his worries preparing for the science test, I listened and asked how I could help.	Janie complained about her brother, so I asked questions to better understand her thoughts about him.
This week I practiced accepting their thoughts by listening and asking curious questions.		
I practiced accepting their feelings by providing support.		
I practiced agreeing to disagree by remaining calm during discussions.		

I practiced equality by showing my friend that they are important to me.		
I honored their wishes by fulfilling them.		
I honored their rights by protecting them.		
I valued their abilities by letting them know I appreciate them.		

24 recognizing safe and unsafe relationships

for you to know

When a relationship is safe, it is emotionally, mentally, and physically safe. This helps you feel secure and able to trust the other person. If you have a relationship that is not a safe place for you—physically, emotionally, or mentally—then you can feel unsafe in all relationships, even the ones that are safe.

When relationships have not felt safe, the alert system in your brain activates to keep you safe. This alert system takes its job very seriously. It sends you signals that danger may be present, telling you to fight, flee, or freeze to protect yourself from harm. It may be triggered by something that reminds you of an unsafe time in your life. Its job is to keep you safe and protect you, which is so important! But if your inner alarm bell has been ringing a lot during your life, sometimes it can be hypervigilant. The protective signal can become overactive, telling you that *all* relationships are unsafe. But you have people in your life who are safe and would not hurt you. It's important to recognize when people are safe. You can help your brain recognize a safe relationship by learning more about what safe people are like. Then you will be able to tell how they are different from unsafe people.

Safe relationships feel comfortable and relaxed, like a shelter amidst the storms of life. You can return to a safe relationship for support, problem solving, and empathy. This person knows, understands, and accepts you. Your thoughts and feelings are validated. You feel like you can truly be yourself because you are valued for who you are.

If you have not experienced a safe relationship, it can be hard to imagine it exists. But it does! Recognizing these traits in another person helps you know you are in a safe relationship. Then you can tell your alert system that everything is okay, that you are okay. Your alert system will calm down and relax, so you can enjoy the relationship.

for you to do

You can protect yourself, and your heart, by recognizing whether someone is safe or unsafe. Look at the relationship traits in the following chart of safe and unsafe characteristics. Think about relationships you have now. Then answer the questions.

Safe relationship traits	Unsafe relationship traits
They listen when I talk and share my thoughts.	They appear annoyed or distracted when I talk. They tell me my thoughts are not important.
They value my feelings and offer me support.	They disregard my feelings and tell me that I shouldn't feel that way.
When I share hard things, they offer me comfort.	When I share hard things, they distance from me emotionally or move away from me physically.
They help me to follow my dreams.	They tell me that my dreams are unimportant.
When I face challenges, they help solve problems with me.	They leave me alone to handle my problems.
They try to identify my needs, physically and emotionally, and meet them.	They ignore my needs, physically or emotionally, and do not help me meet them.
They consistently show up when I need them.	They come and go in my life. I can't count on them.
They are dependable and do what they say they will do.	They make empty promises and do not follow through.

Consider the following questions.

Have you ever met anyone with safe relationship traits? Think back over your lifetime. Maybe it was a teacher, a friend's parent, a friend, a grandparent, or an extended family member like an uncle or aunt. How did that relationship feel to you?

_____

_____

_____

Is there anyone in your life now who has these safe relationship traits? If so, write their name down. Then describe a plan to spend more time with them. This will give you more experiences with safe relationships and will help your brain recognize safe people.

_____

_____

_____

If you cannot identify anyone currently in your life who is a safe person, think about the safe traits from the previous chart and spend time this week observing the people around you. Who could have these traits? Write down their names and describe why you think they may be safe people.

_____

_____

_____

You may have safe people around you, but your brain struggles to recognize them. Your alert system may be always at work, trying to keep you safe. So observe teachers, school staff, extended family members, neighbors, and other students in your classes. You may be surprised to learn that you actually know safe people! You just haven't developed relationships with them yet.

more to do

Part of having safe relationships with others is being a safe person yourself. People who are safe look for other safe people to form relationships with. Look again at the chart of safe and unsafe traits. Notice which side of the list applies to your own traits. Are you a safe person or an unsafe person in relationships? Maybe you are a mix of both lists. Taking stock of your relationship traits can help create a list of traits to work on developing as you continue your journey toward healthy relationships.

List the safe relationship traits you recognize in yourself.

_____

_____

_____

List the unsafe relationship traits you recognize in yourself.

_____

_____

_____

Think about how those unsafe relationship traits may be impacting your relationships. Give an example of what happens when someone does not feel safe around you.

_____

_____

_____

Consider how you can begin working on becoming a safer person. What would your next steps be? Sometimes it means doing the opposite of what you are doing now. For example, if you realized you dismiss the thoughts of others, take time to intentionally listen to another and consider their thoughts. That's a good step in the right direction to change that trait. Write down three steps you can take.

1. _____

2. _____

3. _____

Choose one trait to work on this week. Once you feel confident of progress in that area, choose another one to work on! Slowly, and surely, you can have safe relationships too.

PART SIX

Attachment in Specific Relationships

25 healthy connections in friendships

for you to know

Who you spend time with shapes who you become as a person. Attachment is fluid, so it changes based on the relationship. If you want to make positive choices and pursue life goals, spend time with people who are already doing those things. You will stay focused and those friends can support you to reach your goals.

Haley has been friends with Josh for most of her life. They play games and watch movies together. Their families are friends, so they share holiday and birthday celebrations. As teenagers, they both got jobs at the same restaurant and worked hard while having fun and laughing together. Haley is kind to others, honest, and always willing to help Josh with homework. This means a lot to Josh.

In high school, Haley has different classes than Josh, and they don't see each other as much during the day. Josh is around other students and begins to make new friends. Haley still sees him at work and when their families get together, but they have different friends at school and are hanging out less and less.

Haley notices that Josh is hanging out with Adam and Cole. They are "cool kids" and Josh says he feels popular when he is with them. Adam is not honest and often blames others when he gets in trouble. Cole is disrespectful to teachers and frequently does not complete classes or homework. They laugh at others, make fun of them, and are disrespectful. Haley is a different type of friend because she does not do any of those things.

One day at work Haley saw Josh being disrespectful to their boss and she was surprised. She tried to talk to him, but Josh told her to mind her own business. A few weeks later, Josh was disrespectful to his boss again and was fired. Haley feels confused because Josh isn't the friend he used to be. Since he started hanging out with Adam and Cole, he has changed. She misses the old Josh but doesn't know how to reach him.

for you to do

Attachment is fluid, it can change. When you spend time with friends who are respectful and trustworthy, in order to connect with them you will act the same way. However, if you spend time with friends who are dishonest and disrespectful, you will begin to behave that way too. When we want to connect with someone, we begin to mirror them. Be careful who you spend time with and mirror, because your attachment style can change in both healthy and unhealthy ways.

Think about the character qualities in friends that are important to you. What do you look for in a friend? Go through this list and circle the characteristics that are important to you, or write in your own.

kind	generous	responsible	brave	honest
hard working	helpful	reliable	careful	intelligent
trustworthy	optimistic	unselfish	considerate	encouraging
accepting	sincere	persistent	determined	caring
forgiving	humorous	organized	flexible	confident
understanding	compassionate	easygoing	creative	good listener
thoughtful	cooperative	motivated	patient	reasonable
dedicated	focused	_____	_____	_____

Now choose the four characteristics that are most important to you.

1. _____ 2. _____

3. _____ 4. _____

Take those character traits and write them in the chart below. Add the names of your friends and explore how their character compares to your thoughts about what a good friend should be.

Name	1. Honest	2. Hard working	3. Encouraging	4. Good listener
Justin	X	X		X
Emma		X	X	X

Name	1._____	2._____	3._____	4._____

more to do

Consider the list of friends and their character traits in the chart. Then answer these questions.

Name the friend who is most like you. (You have similar traits.)

_____

Identify the friend who is least like you. (You have different traits, or they have traits opposite to those you value in a friend.)

_____

Who gives you the most support through encouragement, problem solving, dependability, and reliability?

_____

Do you support one friend more than others? Who do you help?

_____

Who will best support you to achieve your goals and dreams? Name a friend who is going in a similar direction as you.

_____

Did you learn anything from this exercise that surprises you? Perhaps it reinforces what you already know about your close friendships. Spending time with people who are going in similar directions in life will help you get there faster! Spending time with friends who have healthy relationships will help you have healthy relationships too.

26 the dating relationship

for you to know

Romantic relationships involve more emotions than friendships do, which is why they can feel euphoric. Large amounts of a hormone called *dopamine* are released at the beginning of a dating relationship because it is new, fun, and exciting. It's important to be ready for these big emotions before you enter a romantic relationship.

A romantic relationship is built in the same way as other relationships: attunement leads to trust and vulnerability, which creates attachment. Romantic relationships that begin as friendships and have a friendship at its base tend to be healthier and more balanced. Meeting each other's needs physically, emotionally, and intellectually within a romantic relationship builds a strong connection.

Physical needs can include going out to eat, giving them a sweater or sweatshirt to wear when they are cold, or keeping them safe when others are bullying or threatening them.

Emotional needs can include listening, validating their feelings, offering them a hug on a hard day, or celebrating an achievement with them.

Intellectual needs can include talking through ideas, opinions, and thoughts, as well as studying together.

These acts build trust and allow you to be emotionally vulnerable. But don't allow your emotions to engage too quickly before trust has been established. Ensure that the person you want to date is trustworthy first.

Yes, building a strong relationship will help you form a secure romantic attachment. It is also important to use emotion regulation and calming techniques. Even positive emotions like excitement and happiness can grow too large to handle. They may need to be calmed. Any time your emotions grow oversized, in any environment, you need to calm them. This happens frequently in romantic relationships because positive hormones are released in large quantities when a romantic relationship begins. If your feelings grow large, you may lose control of them, which can lead to poor decision making. This is because you can make decisions with your feelings instead of your logic. While at times it is beneficial to use your feelings to make a decision, you do not want to make a decision completely based on feelings. Logic is your ability to rationalize, reason, compare pros and cons, consider possible outcomes, and weigh consequences. When you stay logical amidst big emotions, you make better choices.

for you to do

When entering a romantic relationship, allow trust to build before engaging all your emotions. This protects your heart from painful disappointment if someone you are attracted to is not trustworthy. Think about how you might build a healthy romantic relationship using attunement to build trust, which leads to vulnerability.

Review the following list of activities. Then, in the following chart, for each attachment-building stage, write the letter of the appropriate activity. This will help you discover ways to build a healthy romantic relationship as you protect your heart by using logic to make good choices.

A. Sharing bigger thoughts

B. Solving problems together

C. Helping each other with homework

D. Sharing bigger feelings

E. Sharing a meal together

F. Talking about our days

G. Seeking emotional support

H. Sharing smaller thoughts and feelings

Relationship timeline	Attachment-building phase	Activities
Beginning of relationship	Attunement	
Growing relationship	Trust	
Stronger relationship	Vulnerability	
Established relationship	Attachment	

*See the answer key at the end of the chapter.

more to do

Sometimes it can feel hard to move slowly and use self-control when you are excited about a new relationship. But taking your time is a way to protect your heart and emotions. Your heart is worth protecting! When you find the right person, someone who is trustworthy, your heart will be safe in their care.

Delaying gratification can be challenging when you want something. Once a person has shown that they are invested in meeting your needs and think you are important enough to put your needs before their wants, the relationship will be healthier. It can be helpful to talk to someone who has been in romantic relationships before to hear about their experiences—both good and bad—and learn from them. You know people who have had romantic relationships before: your parents and caregivers! This week interview a parent or caregiver about their experience with romantic relationships. Ask the following questions and write what you can learn from them. To interview multiple people, download the questions at http://www.newharbinger.com/48725.

What happened on your best date?

_____

_____

_____

What happened on your worst date?

_____

_____

_____

When did you meet my your partner and how did you begin your relationship?

_____

_____

_____

How did you build a healthy romantic relationship? What are some things you did?

_____

_____

_____

Is there anything you would never do again in a romantic relationship?

_____

_____

_____

Do you have advice that can help me have a good dating relationship?

_____

_____

_____

Should I avoid anything in a dating relationship?

_____

_____

_____

What do you wish for me in a dating relationship?

_____

_____

_____

If you feel comfortable, continue the conversation with your parents or caregivers and tell them your plans for dating, or share the chart you completed. Consider their responses to your plans and ask them what their thoughts are about your romantic relationships.

Answer Key

Attunement: C, E, F

Trust: H

Vulnerability: A, D

Attachment: B, G

for you to know

If you have big feelings of excitement and happiness when a relationship begins, you can expect big feelings of sadness and disappointment if the relationship ends. The stress it creates may release the hormone *adrenaline*, which can cause more distress.

A breakup is a loss. You may experience feelings of grief and sadness. When you have reached the point of trust and vulnerability, you likely shared emotions with this person. So the end of that relationship can feel especially painful. The emotional intensity of the connection in a romantic relationship is unlike any other relationship. After a breakup, feelings of hopelessness and helplessness can seem to take over. But emotions are temporary, they do pass, and different emotions will take their place. You can cope with those feelings while you are waiting for them to pass. It can help to have a "breakup plan" before you even start a relationship. Then you are prepared for the large feelings you may experience, if or when the relationship ends. Broken attachments, if not properly healed, can cause us to avoid new relationships.

When you experience a breakup, recall the purpose of dating. With each experience, you can refine what you are looking for in a partner and learn more about relationships. You learn things from every person you spend time with, which helps shape what you look for in the next relationship.

Jess is going through a breakup. While her feelings are overwhelming and she is experiencing pain, she is also taking stock of the meaning the relationship had for her. She learned that she likes being in a relationship with someone who is funny and also sensitive, organized, and responsible. She also learned that she does not like dating someone who is self-centered and sarcastic. She will apply these preferences to her search for a new romantic relationship.

for you to do

Making a "breakup plan" can help you be prepared. You can take care of yourself and your emotions in ways that reduce anxiety and depression. You can also adjust your plan if some things in your plan are not helpful or you find other things that are more helpful. For example, Jess found that she likes to talk to her best friend about her feelings. But she doesn't like to engage social media because it reminds her of her ex. Identify the people, places, and things that can support you. Think about coping skills that can bring you peace.

Supportive people: Write the names of three people, along with their phone numbers, who you can contact for support. These are people you can talk to and enjoy.

1. _____

2. _____

3. _____

Supportive places: Write down three supportive places where you like to go. These places bring you peace and make you feel good vibes. It may be a place you go to volunteer and give back, or a place that is beautiful like a park or lake. It could also be a relative's house or a special location that holds happy memories.

1. _____

2. _____

3. _____

Supportive things: Circle the coping skills from the following list that bring you peace and lift your spirit. There are two types of coping skills: those that calm you when you're angry or afraid, and those that lift you up when you are feeling low. After a breakup, you need coping skills that will lift you up! Try them out now, before you need them, to see which ones bring you the most peace.

Playing in sand	Deep breathing	Petting my pet
Coloring	Drinking water	Fidgeting
Soaking in a bubble bath	Cold or warm showering	Baking or cooking
Watching a favorite show	Drawing	Crafting
Hugging	Walking	Organizing
Watching funny videos	Helping someone else	Writing in a journal
Napping	Exercising	Playing sports
Reading a book	Planning a fun outing	Listening to a favorite song

more to do

If you have already experienced a breakup or two, complete the following exercise to think about what lessons you are taking away from those relationships. Each relationship leaves you with something. Maybe you learned something you liked, or something you didn't like. You may have learned from the relationship: the way you built it, acted in it, or ended it. Perhaps you gained insight into yourself, either positive or negative, and the way you function in romantic relationships. If you have not yet had a romantic relationship, then save this exercise for after your first breakup. For now, know that you will be taking something away from all your relationships.

What are the things you liked about this person (and will look for in future partners)?

_____

_____

_____

What are the things you didn't like about this person (and want to avoid in future partners)?

_____

_____

_____

What are the things you learned about yourself in this relationship?

_____

_____

_____

What about this relationship worked well for you (that you would repeat in future relationships)?

_____

_____

_____

What about this relationship did not work (and you would not repeat in future relationships)?

_____

_____

_____

for you to know

Modeling works both ways. For years you've watched and learned from your parents' relationship styles. Now that you have learned about healthy relationships, you can bring change to your family by modeling healthy relationship traits.

At the beginning of this workbook, you learned how relationships start. You looked at what your parents taught you, through modeling, about attachment styles and relationship skills. You may have identified that they taught you healthy ways of interacting in relationships with others. You may have identified that your parents modeled some unhealthy traits that you now exhibit as well and want to work on revising.

It's important to view your parents and their relationship skills through a lens of grace. They are likely doing the best they can with the understanding of relationships that your grandparents modeled for them. Attachment styles can be passed down through generations. Unless someone intentionally looks at their attachment style and assesses whether or not it is healthy, like you have done, nothing will change. The way your family interacts will continue to be the same. But once you become aware, you can choose to begin working on healthier relationship traits. By exploring and learning about this now, you can intentionally pass healthy attachment and relationship skills on to the next generation.

What you have learned about relationships will change the way you interact with others. At school, at home, and in the community, you will become a different person as you apply what you have learned. Others may notice changes in the way you treat them and how you allow them to treat you. As you change the ways you are interacting, you will be modeling what healthy relationships look like to others. This may change some of your friendships and family relationships. You may be able to teach others what healthy relationships and attachments are—not necessarily by what you say, but by what you do.

There may be some people who will not appreciate the changes that you are making. They may not understand why you are changing and what it means for their relationship with you. There will be others who will encourage you and support you as you strive for healthy attachments. Remember that you are making these changes for yourself, not anyone else. You are making these changes to find more fulfilling and meaningful relationships. You are working to make your relationships safe places for both yourself and others. As you become more balanced in your relationships, others may approach you and want to know what you have learned. Be ready to share what you know! You can bring change to everyone around you by modeling healthy attachment!

for you to do

Think about the things you have learned in this workbook. What do you want to share with those around you? Consider the following list of people and think about what you want to share with them about what you've learned. Remember, you might not share using words. Instead, you can use your behaviors to model and share more than words alone could tell.

What do I want to share with my parents or caregivers about what I've learned?

_____

_____

_____

What do I want to share with friends about what I've learned?

_____

_____

_____

What do I want to share with others about what I've learned?

_____

_____

_____

more to do

Think about what you have learned on this journey into attachment. What will you take with you as you go forward? What skills do you want to continue working on and intentionally incorporate into your life? List them below.

1. _____

2. _____

3. _____

4. _____

5. _____

6. _____

7. _____

8. _____

Change happens when you are aware and intentional about applying what you have learned. These relationship skills will be with you as you move forward into your adult life. If you find yourself becoming stuck in a relationship, and your skills are not working, revisit this book and review the things you learned. It can be a road map to healthy connections and attachments for years to come.

The more healthy relationships you have, the more your brain will recognize them and move you toward them. If a relationship becomes unhealthy, you can work to bring balance and safety to it—as long as the other person is willing as well. You can also review healthy relationship skills, put them into practice, and see if the other person responds. Relationships are living things that need to be continuously cultivated to stay alive. Tend to them well and you will reap a crop of meaningful and fulfilling attachments!

your journey ahead

When you connect with others, secure attachment is healthy attachment. This type of relationship provides a safe place in the world where you feel accepted and understood. Having a securely attached relationship means that you have someone to turn to for support, problem solving, and love.

Attunement is the beginning of a healthy relationship, meaning that you and another person are focused on meeting each other's needs. One of our most important needs is love, and relationships meet that need! When another person sees you, hears you, understands you, and cares for you, they will want to meet your needs.

This leads to trust, as you trust the friend who is meeting your needs, and they trust you as you meet their needs. With trust comes vulnerability and the sharing of thoughts and feelings with confidence that they will be respected and valued.

This is something that we all crave and need, but not every relationship provides this depth of meaningful connection. You can have relationships that provide a comfort zone or home base that you can turn to when life gets hard. The result is secure attachment, a safe place for you to be *you*!

acknowledgments

My parents, Brian and Cindy, modeled attachment for me as my first relationships and created my own internal working model of relationships. Thank you for the gift of loving relationships! My nieces and nephews will soon travel this path: Ali, Elijah, Levi, Jeremy, Lydia, Silas, and Quinn. May you find healthy and secure attachments at home that give you the wings to fly! I especially appreciate Jesus for lovingly attaching to me so that I can lovingly attach to others.

To the amazing team at New Harbinger, who supportively and encouragingly walked beside me through this process, thank you for your patience and constructive feedback! Those who have studied attachment created the foundation I stand firmly on. John Bowlby started it all with his discovery of the internal working model. Harry Harlow and his monkeys, who sought love over food, showed the importance of relationships. Mary Ainsworth and Mary Main gave us attachment styles and a better understanding of connection. Dan Siegel paired attachment with neurobiology to explain why relationships are so important. Bruce Perry uses brain scans to actually show how this works. And Karyn Purvis and David Cross developed trust-based relational intervention (TBRI) to teach parents the best attachment-based ways to connect with their children. Thank you for your contributions!

Christina Reese, PhD, is a licensed clinical therapist who specializes in attachment theory. She has extensive experience with attachment trauma and adoption, working on connecting families and building stronger relationships. Reese provides educational seminars across the country on attachment and trauma in children and families, and is author of *Attachment, Puzzle Pieces, The Attachment Connection,* and *Trauma and Attachment.*

Foreword writer **David A. Crenshaw, PhD, ABPP,** is clinical director of the Children's Home of Poughkeepsie, NY, and adjunct faculty at Marist College. He has authored several books on child and adolescent therapy, child abuse and trauma, and resilience in children.